Changing Roles of Financial Management
Getting Close to the Business

Acknowledgments

The authors would like to thank Bob Moore, Executive Director of the Financial Executives Institute (now retired); Roland Laing, Research Director of Financial Executives Research Foundation; and Frank Spiegel, Steering Committee Chairman for this project. We also want to thank the individuals at the six firms who participated in the research—those who have served on the project's steering committee as well as those interviewed: Charlie Cosgrove of Merck; Jim Meenan, Marlin Pickett, and John McEnvoy of AT&T; Dave Barry and Dale Hathaway of Ford; Roger Roberts of 3M; Gail Littleton of Boeing; and Marjorie Marker of Citicorp.

Changing Roles of Financial Management
Getting Close to the Business

Patrick J. Keating
San Jose State University

Stephen F. Jablonsky
Pennsylvania State University

A Publication of
Financial Executives Research Foundation

Financial Executives Research Foundation
10 Madison Avenue, P.O. Box 1938
Morristown, New Jersey 07962-1938

International Standard Book Number 0–910586–78–0
Library of Congress Catalog Card Number 90–081172
Printed in the United States of America

First Printing

Financial Executives Research Foundation is the research affiliate of Financial Executives
Institute. The basic purpose of the Foundation is to conduct research and publish infor-
mative material in the field of business management, with particular emphasis on the practices of financial management and its evolving role in the management of business.

About the Authors

Patrick J. Keating is an Associate Professor of Business Administration at San Jose State University. He recently completed his Ph.D. at The Pennsylvania State University. Dr. Keating holds an undergraduate degree in electrical engineering from Penn State and a master's degree in public policy analysis from the University of Michigan. His professional experience includes work in budget analysis, systems development and research administration. His research interests focus on shifting patterns of management communication and financial control as strategic adaptions to globalization and shifting norms of workplace organization. He is studying the impact of national and organizational culture on the organization and management of corporate financial work.

Stephen F. Jablonsky is an Associate Professor of Accounting and Management Information Systems and Kellogg Faculty Fellow in the College of Business Administration, The Pennsylvania State University. Dr. Jablonsky teaches financially-based management communication and control systems in the Penn State MBA program, Penn State Executive Education Programs and in-house management education programs.

In addition to the field study based research reported in this monograph, Dr. Jablonsky is interested in how financial controls fit into different management operating philosophies across cultures. He is also interested in the impact of individual psychological preferences on the acceptance of change in management control systems.

Dr Jablonsky held several administrative positions at the University of Illinois prior to joining the faculty at Penn State. He has written articles for *Organizational Behavior and Human Performance, Socio-Economic Planning Sciences, Strategic Management Journal, Academy of Management Review, Accounting Organizations and Society*, among others, as well as having developed the management information systems for the American Symphony Orchestra and the Pennsylvania Department of Aging.

Field Research Coordinating Committee

AT&T
James J. Meenan
Vice President-
  Financial Operations & Systems

Marlin Pickett
Division Manager
Financial Planning

The Boeing Company
Arthur H. Lowell
Vice President &
Controller Assistant

Gayle R. Littleton
Controller-Defense Projects

Citicorp
Roger W. Trupin
Vice President

Marjorie B. Marker
Vice President
(Citibank, N.A.)

Ford Motor Company
Dale M. Hathaway
Project Supervisor-
  Planning & Development

Dave Barry
Manager-Financial Process

Merck & Company
Francis H. Spiegel, Jr
Senior Vice President

Charles V. Cosgrove
Director, Controller Operations

Minnesota Mining & Manufacturing
Roger W. Roberts
Vice President - Finance

Francis H. Spiegel, Jr
Committee Chairman
Merck & Company

Contents

Foreword

New FERF Series on Innovative Management

FERF has launched several new projects that will compile the experiences of companies that have made innovative changes in the way they are managed financially. Most of the projects will use field research methods, that is case studies. The stories will describe how innovation and change were achieved and highlight:

□   What circumstances lead to the need for change.

□   Who nurtured and sponsored the idea and initiatives.

□   How the idea was converted to plans and actions.

□   How the new management practices were implemented.

□   Are the new ways effective?

Each book in the series will have its own style and feel. Not only will the topics differ, but the unique mix of cases in each research report will provide an array of ideas and rich narratives of the circumstances and actions that enable innovation and change to flourish in a financial organization. The primary objectives of these research studies are to aid financial executives in envisioning ways to improve the effectiveness of the financial functions in their own companies and to demonstrate the approaches and practices that enable them to promote and encourage innovation and manage change.

As the first book in the series, *Changing Roles of Financial Management: Getting Close to the Business* sets a high standard and challenge for other projects. It leads off by hitting at the first-order questions of who are the customers of financial work and how well are they served. It recommends that the financial professional should be a direct participant in the game of business as coach or player—on the field and out of the front office. The education, recruitment, training, and development of this type of financial executive will be different than current ways.

We hope that in this book and others in this series, you will find new insights and fresh ideas about the evolving role of the financial function and the opportunities for growth as financial executives.

Roland L. Laing
FERF Director of Research
30 May, 1990

Executive Summary

In what ways is financial work changing in American corporations? How is it being influenced by the pressures of global competition and government regulations? Is it true that too much managing-by-the-numbers has suppressed innovation and creativity? What impact is new technology having on financial operations? Are our universities properly training people to work effectively in today's corporate financial environment?

These are some of the many questions we sought to answer in this field research study. The study focuses on patterns of both variation and change. It describes the various approaches for organizing and managing financial work and synthesizes the changes occurring in financial managements of a select group of companies. The new trend entails integrating financial work into the fabric of the business. The individual case studies will describe how each company is moving to get financial work close to the business and making changes in its management philosophy, allocation of resources, use of technology, and development of human resources.

The study carefully and intimately examines financial work in six major corporations—AT&T, Boeing, Citicorp, Ford, Merck, and 3M. We selected these firms because of their reputations for competitive excellence or their perceived ability to adapt to changes in the business climate. They typify a cross section of strategic industries, including aerospace, automobiles, banking, pharmaceuticals, and information processing and telecommunications.

The Issues Facing Financial Executives

These are challenging times for corporate financial executives. They are expected to accomplish more with fewer resources. They are expected to provide more sophisticated financial services to their corporations' business units. But they are also required to reduce their personnel through the increased use of computer technology.

The intensity of global competition and the constant change in government regulations have also had their impact. Financial executives are being asked to become more involved in business operations, while maintaining the integrity of the corporate financial system.

In addition, financial executives are often criticized for managing-by-the-numbers. It is said that the financial perspective places too much emphasis on paper profits instead of on people and production, to the detriment of long-term, value-adding activities and corporate vitality. (For instance, see Hayes and Abernathy, 1980; Reich, 1983; Peters and Austin, 1985; and, most recently, Detouzos et al., 1989.)

Critics argue that in managing-by-the-numbers, resources invested in the financial function have been paying negative returns, because the costs of financial control have exceeded the benefits. Thus, financial executives are being challenged to do things differently, as well as achieving more with less.

Method Used in the Study

We used a case study method in conducting our research. It was chosen over the survey method so concrete examples of variation and change in individual firms could be obtained. We expected it to generate a richer understanding of patterns and changes in financial work. We also believed that financial executives, as well as business analysts and educators, could benefit from an exploration based on concrete examples.

Financial executives directly responsible for initiating change were interviewed. This gave us the subjective information. We also collected objective information found in "hard data" about the changes in size and structure of the financial function over the past decade. Our findings are based primarily on the interviews. The hard data served more as a backdrop confirming the statements made by the financial executives.

We asked the financial executives, and other members of corporate management when appropriate, to discuss the changes going on in the organization of financial work. We asked them to tell us about their criteria for success of the financial function and if these criteria had changed over time. We also asked for the basis of changes and what change meant for the management of financial work.

The Findings

Our major findings were:

1. Major changes have taken place in the character and cost of financial work.

2. Financial work at various corporations falls into three distinct patterns, or orientations.

3. There is a distinct trend toward the competitive-team orientation in financial work. This trend, which stresses streamlined integration of the financial perspective in business strategy and operations, is consistent with the broader movement in corporate America toward leaner, more flexible, and more knowledge-based forms of organization.

These three findings led us to develop a conceptual model that we believe will help any corporation to assess its financial orientation and lead it to beneficial change.

Following are some of the details of the findings and the conceptual model.

Character and Cost of Financial Work

We can group the character and cost of financial work into these broad categories:

☐ Firms are either reallocating their existing resources or investing in additional resources to achieve the greater sophistication of financial systems and services needed to support the management of global strategy.

☐ In some firms, the walls between finance and line management are being torn down. Financial control is becoming a shared responsibility for all members of the management team. This shared responsibility is creating a new ethic of financial communication and information sharing. Line managers are now being required to become more financially literate, while financial managers are being required to share information, to communicate, and to become more business literate. Furthermore, financial executives are being asked to accept more responsibility for the achievement of "non-financial" aspects of business performance, such as product quality and customer service.

☐ Firms with financial systems based on elaborate functions or bureaucracy are striving to simplify and streamline their systems, to become more product-oriented and customer-oriented. Firms that already have integrated financial systems are reducing their administrative costs through the use of state-of-the-art computer technology. Resources no longer needed for administrative tasks are being allocated to support more sophisticated analysis.

The Orientations of Financial Work

These changes in the character and cost of financial work are grounded in a broader shift in corporate culture. Hence, our second major finding—that there are three distinct orientations to financial work. These orientations reflect management's philosophy for operating the company and for organizing the workplace.

Command-and-Control Orientation: This orientation of financial work is found in firms with a traditional functional organization and a chain-of-command style of management. It stresses corporate oversight, operating efficiency, and conservation of corporate resources. In these firms, the financial organization provides an independent financial assessment of business plans.

Conformance Orientation: It is found in organizations that do a sizable amount of business with the government or those subject to pervasive government regulation. The financial function is organized as a bureaucracy, with fixed routines for processing financial information. This orientation is subject to external accountability, technical compliance with rules and regulations, and technical bookkeeping procedures. The financial organization in these firms is the repository for all the technical and procedural knowledge required for compliance with externally imposed regulations.

Competitive-Team Orientation: Firms with this type of financial orientation are ones where financial work is focused on the market, those that integrate financial work into the business organization, and those that use the matrix style of management. Companies with this orientation stress commitment to using financial analysis to enhance the firms' core competiveness and strategic competitiveness through customer service, financial leadership, value-added involvement with the management team, and a sophisticated knowledge of the business.

The six companies interviewed in this study have either moved from one orientation to another or fall between two of the orientations.

The Trend Toward the Competitive-Team Orientation

Our third major finding was that four of the six firms in this study are following a distinct trend toward the competitive-team orientation and related patterns of financial work. In those firms that have undergone major changes in competition or regulations, the change has been away from either a strong command-and-control orientation or a conformance orientation. The change was precipitated either by competition in the marketplace or by changes in government regulation.

Where we have found the shift to the competitive-team orientation, the financial executives we interviewed were most helpful in contrasting the new orientation with the previous command-and-control or conformance orientation.

To shift toward the competitive-team orientation, people have to change the way they think about how they contribute to the success of their firms. This means they move away from being an independent third party or custodian of the accounts and become a client-oriented professional (both internal and external clients) with an in-depth knowledge of the business.

To make the transition to a team-oriented financial organization, a company must change its operating philosophy. It must reorient the financial function; it must make interrelated changes in the norms of success. For example, as the Ford case demonstrates, the competitive-team orientation tends to eliminate unnecessarily redundant financial control systems. In the Merck case, the competitive-team orientation commits the organization to upgrade the sophistication of all members of the financial organization. The Citicorp case shows that a firm doesn't need to undergo a severe economic crisis to force a change in orientation.

Figure 1 shows the three orientations for the financial function as interlocking circles. In a command-and-control environment, the financial function is oriented internally to the corporate hierarchy. Information flows vertically up and down the chain of command in a mode of oversight and review. In a conformance environment, the financial function is oriented to processing accounting transactions according to externally imposed rules and regulations. Information flows into the financial function with little or no management information flowing back into the organization. In a competitive-team environment, the financial function is oriented to customer markets (both external and internal). Information flows laterally and informally throughout the organization. We'll discuss this concept more fully in Chapter 4.

FIGURE 1 Orientation of Financial Management

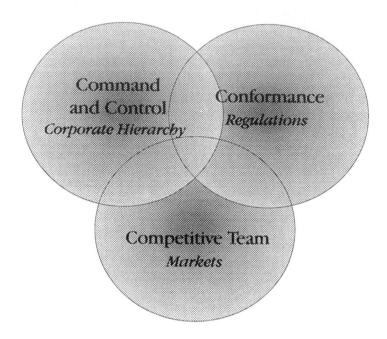

Although most firms have elements of corporate financial work that are anchored in each of the three orientations, they will have a dominant pattern of orientation and direction of change. Each of the financial organizations included in this study is required to provide command-and-control, conformance, and competitive-team types of services to a greater or lesser degree. However, different patterns of variation and change are associated with a particular dominant orientation.

The Conceptual Model

A major outcome of this research was the development of a conceptual model. We believe it will help assess a financial organization's current orientation. It can tell financial executives how they might start thinking about changing their organization if they face challenges similar to the firms included in this study.

The conceptual model embeds the three orientations to financial work within a broader organizational context. Each firm's case study is told as a story using the conceptual framework. By using this common framework to tell each story, common themes cutting across all firms tend to emerge without taking away any of the unique history, management philosophy, and competitive contingencies of each firm.

The Educational Challenge

If the changes going on within these six firms are representative of the broader changes occurring in American industry, then we have found that financial executives are rethinking how their financial functions are organized and managed.

As educators, we see a demand for more sophisticated financial professionals that is not being met by the current business school curricula. Functional disciplinary boundaries (chimneys, walls, transoms), characteristic of the command-and-control orientations, which are crumbling in some firms, are still being reinforced with concrete within the business schools. The long-standing distinctions made within business schools between finance and accounting, between financial managers and auditors, and between theory and practice result in an education that is inadequate to meet the needs of financial executives facing a changing business environment and changing norms of the workplace.

Organization of This Book

There are two sections to this monograph. Section A presents background material, issues that have emerged from the study, and our overall conclusions. Chapter 1 presents a capsule summary of what we believe is an emergent trend in corporate financial work—the competitive-team orientation. Chapter 2 presents the broader debate concerning the current relevance of the financial organization in the light of the changes in global competition and government regulation. We give specific attention to the controversy over managing-by-the-numbers. In Chapter 3 we show the change in the character, cost, and orientation of financial work. Chapter 4 develops the full conceptual model that has emerged from the study. Chapter 5 presents a set of challenges that we and the project steering committee believe must be addressed by the educational community.

Section B consists of the six case studies: Ford, Merck, Citicorp, 3M, AT&T, and Boeing. We document the unique history, corporate culture, and competitive and regulatory contingencies that have influenced the rate of change and its direction within the financial function. The Appendix describes the research design and methodology that guided the entire research study.

We encourage the reader to read the chapters in the order they are written. To gain an appreciation of the overall patterns of variation and change that cut across all six case studies, the reader is better served by reading the earlier chapters before reading the case studies. However, each individual case does stand on its own. Thus, if one case study holds particular interest for a reader, it can be read and appreciated without having to invest a great deal of time with the other chapters.

Section A

Contents

1

The Emergence of the Competitive-Team Orientation

If most American companies face the same challenges as the six firms in our study, then they will be interested in the changes taking place these days in the organization and management of financial work. Business researchers will also be concerned.

We have observed the emergence of a competitive-team orientation to financial work in such firms as Ford, AT&T, and Citicorp, where either competitive crisis or deregulation has set the stage for major changes in the financial organization. In Merck, Boeing, and 3M, where changes in the business environment have been more gradual or less dramatic, the competitive-team orientation exists to a greater or lesser degree.

The most dramatic changes in financial organizations have been found where there has been either:

☐ A movement away from an arm's-length, independent, third-party relationship with the business units, or

☐ A movement away from a technical, bureaucratic operation with little or no involvement with the business units.

Each of these firms has been moving toward a financial organization that emphasizes value-added involvement with the business units. Financial professionals are expected to contribute to the bottom line within the business units, while maintaining the integrity of the financial system on behalf of the corporation. In these cases, the financial organizations are "getting closer to the business."

Before developing the essential features of the competitive-team orientation, it might be useful to identify the three types of changes that are occurring within the financial organizations included in this study.

The Character and Cost of Financial Work

Each firm included in the study is making changes in the character and cost of financial work in its own way. The changes fall into three categories:

- Firms are either reallocating existing resources or investing additional resources to increase the sophistication of financial analysis and financial systems services used to support global competitive strategy.

- In some firms, the walls between finance and line management are being torn down. Financial control is becoming a shared responsibility for all members of the management team. This shared responsibility is creating a new ethic of financial communication and information sharing. Line managers are now being required to become more financially literate, while financial managers are being required to share information, to communicate, and to become more business literate. Furthermore, financial executives are being asked to accept more responsibility for the achievement of "non-financial" aspects of business performance, such as product quality and customer service.

- Firms with elaborate functionally- and/or bureaucratically-based financial systems are striving to simplify and streamline their systems to become more product- and customer-oriented. Firms with integrated financial systems are reducing their administrative costs by using state-of-the-art computer technology. Resources thus freed-up are being reallocated to support more sophisticated analysis.

Some firms are making all three of these changes at once. They are the firms that appear to be making the most dramatic shifts to the competitive-team orientation. Firms closer to the command-and-control orientation or the conformance orientation do not seem to place the same emphasis on open communication and full integration into the business units.

The Trend Toward the Competitive-Team Orientation to Financial Work

To fully appreciate the nature of these changes in the character and cost of financial work, one must take a step back and look at the changes that are occurring in management operating philosophies.

There are many terms that convey what the competitive-team orientation is all about. Included are "customer service," "leading-edge," or "sitting at the decision table." But, in our opinion, the phrase "getting close to the business," best captures the essence and spirit of the competitive-team orientation. It is difficult to be involved if you are totally independent. It is also difficult to be involved if you are physically and organizationally assigned to a remote location within the bureaucracy. Involvement and participation in managing the business are key features of the competitive-team orientation.

Within the team context, a financial manager must be involved in the business and, at the same time, be able to adopt a broader corporate perspective. The hallmark of the financial professional is the ability to accept dual responsibilities—to be accountable to the business units for financial analysis, and at the corporate level be accountable for maintaining the integrity of the financial system.

The competitive-team orientation in a corporation is similar to a competitive team in a sport such as football. Championship teams emerge from an effective blend of on-the-field and off-the-field excellence. First and foremost, it is the players who produce the win on the field. But the players must have effective support from the coaches. The coaches, in turn, need a strong franchise that provides the resources to acquire the players and off-the-field talent to make the organization a financial success. We believe that the unique challenge facing the financial professional within a competitive-team orientation is learning how to become a player and a coach. This is not an insignificant task when individuals have been trained in school and continued professionally to be scorekeepers or independent commentators.

Getting close to the business means getting on the field as part of the management team. As a player, you are involved in the game. As a coach, you are on the sidelines or in the coaching booth to support the players. In either case, you are not a commentator hired by the newsmedia to provide an independent view of the game, nor are you locked in a back office counting gate receipts. You are a player or coach directly participating in the outcome of the game.

Within the competitive-team orientation, members of the financial organization are committed first and foremost to help create value in the marketplace, not simply conserving or counting the value created by other members of the organization. To do so, financial managers must become players and committed students of the business. Detached financial analysis carries no credibility with those spilling their guts on the field. When owners of sports teams forget that championships are won on the field, or that success is determined in the marketplace, fans lose interest and customers go elsewhere. Most of the financial executives interviewed in this study are being asked to get back on the field—get closer to the business.

Neither the significance nor the difficulty of this challenge should be underestimated. Continuing with the sports analogy, how many front-office personnel have the skills or predisposition to be players or coaches? Yet, financial executives and professional staff are being challenged to make this move.

To get close to the business, a financial executive needs a change in the mind-set that centers around the concept of control. Within the competitive-team orientation, control is seen as being a shared responsibility between the players and coaches (on the field) and general managers and owners (off the field). Financial control is no longer the sole province of the financial organization. Nor can it be adequately defined in impersonal policy and procedures manuals. Control is a responsibility shared by all members of the management team.

The Ford case presents a graphic statement of the change in philosophy required to support market-oriented team players. The company is shifting its functionally-oriented financial organization, which in many cases operated on a confrontation basis, into more of a matrix organization that is integrated into the business operations.

In a functional organization, chimneys are built. Information (smoke) flows vertically and enters the atmosphere only at a very high level. In a competitive-team environment, there is no place for chimneys. Financial information must flow to the people who own the resources and are responsible for the costs. In moving toward a team management concept, Ford is trying to push the appropriate ownership of resources down and out into the organization and provide improved financial services to these new owners.

Case Study Examples
of the Competitive-Team Orientation

The Ford case presents a number of concrete examples of change. It has been extremely useful in showing the emergence of a competitive-team orientation. Ford's program of process simplification is possibly the best example of a change in the financial organization. Based initially on studies conducted on site at Mazda, Ford is simplifying its financial systems as part of a firm-wide strategy to reduce administrative costs. However, it was not clear in the beginning how the strategy of process simplification could be implemented while still maintaining sound internal control. Ford found that traditional views of cost control, which are characteristic of a command-and-control orientation, had to be modified within a team orientation. Consequently, responsibility for costs is now being embedded into the operating systems themselves and responsibility for cost control has been shifted to line managers. Ford maintains that this shift has not weakened controls. The company's financial managers are finding that many historical financial practices must be challenged as they move toward process simplification.

In one form of the competitive-team model, the financial professional is on the field and in the game as a player. Good examples are the Citicorp, Ford, and Merck cases. In another form of the competitive-team model, the financial professional is a coach supporting the players, as in the cases of 3M and AT&T. However, even in those firms where the competitive-team orientation predominates, the financial organization still has command-and-control (stewardship) and conformance (score keeping) responsibilities.

While the emergence of the team-oriented financial professional does not imply that the stewardship responsibilities of the financial organization are no longer relevant or valued, the shift to the competitive-team orientation does place control within a new ethic of trust and communication. The competitive-team orientation promotes open communication in place of a need-to-know policy, with very few people needing to know anything. The financial professional exercises the stewardship function within an organizational climate that presumes openness, trust and collective self-discipline as the norm, not the exception. Providing the fiscal conscience of the team is one of the skills the financial professional brings to the team.

With a competitive-team orientation, the legitimacy of financial professionals is not based on their off-the-field position as members of the front or back office. Rather, it is based upon active, effective participation in forming and executing competitive strategy. This calls for an in-depth understanding of business operations and the competitive and regulatory environment. For example, the AT&T executives talked about helping management to understand the "real economics of the business." People at Merck talked about helping managers to understand the language of risk and return and then to apply the risk/return decision-making logic to new R&D programs. At Ford, they talked about moving financial analysis upstream to support competitive analysis. At 3M, we heard about the need to "get back to the business" and provide more financial consulting services. And at Boeing, they talked of building a financial perspective into the commercial business through design-to-cost teams.

In all of the interviews that emphasized a team concept, financial people were expected to think like a player or coach on the field, not as a scorekeeper or statistician. They all stressed the need for better financial leadership throughout all levels of the financial organization. For example, Merck and 3M executives emphasized the growing scope of the divisional controller's role as chief financial advisor to the firm's global product managers. Such advice must be given from the perspective of someone who is on the field, not from the perspective of an independent, uninvolved third party.

Where top management expects the financial function to get close to the business, the senior financial executives are the role models for the new breed of financial professionals. Merck's senior financial executives, for example, project an image and vision of a financial function that helps create value in addition to helping conserve what was created by others in the past. Merck has created a culture within the financial function that is oriented to creating competitive advantage for the organization.

Merck has a reputation for being a leading-edge R&D firm in the pharmaceutical field. However, R&D does not stop at the edge of the laboratory door. The firm's financial executives believe that the financial organization has its own frontiers. The Merck case study describes the company's R&D planning model, which was developed by the financial organization. The R&D planning model is an innovative financial tool that integrates the latest computer technology with the latest research advances in financial modeling. Merck's management believes that the R&D planning model has had a measurable impact on the firm's bottom line and has been instrumental in establishing the value of the financial organization to its research scientists. In a very real sense, innovative tools and products, such as the R&D model, represent specialized knowledge that gives the firm a competitive advantage.

Before we move on to Chapter 2, we must reinforce the point that the competitive-team orientation demands more open communication than required by the other two orientations. In a competitive-team environment, all managers need to know the financial implications of their actions. Barriers to communication must come down. In Ford, the chimney mentality throughout the organization was—and still is—a constant threat to the competitive-team orientation. In Boeing, they refer to "throwing the engineering drawings over the wall" to materiel and finance. In AT&T, transoms provide the barriers to communication. In Citicorp, communication was impeded by long, narrow corridors and closed doors. In Merck and 3M, imaginary lines between the controller and treasury created very real barriers to communication. In all instances, where there is a movement toward the competitive-team concept, there is also movement toward a more open flow of communication, more open office space, and more movement to be closer to the businesses.

In Chapter 2, we present our rationale for undertaking this study of the financial function within corporate America. The issues of global competition, government regulation and the essence of the debate over management-by-the-numbers will be discussed in some depth.

2

The Changing Nature of Corporate Financial Work: Context and Criticisms

Changes in the way firms are managed and controlled are on the way. The changes stem from intense global competition, changing government regulations, and technological innovation. Every day new standards of the best industrial practices are being set by leading-edge American firms. They must now compete in product innovation, product quality, customer service, and efficiency. Yet, as the competitive stakes have risen, many well-established American companies have been caught unprepared. While they rest on the laurels of their past performance and operate under outmoded management philosophies, they have been slow to adapt to the new imperatives of global competition.

In her book *When Giants Learn to Dance*, Rosabeth Kanter argues that global competition is forcing corporations away from bureaucratic and inefficient organizational structures that stifle innovation and entrepreneurial activity. The new corporate imperatives for innovation and efficiency have multiplied the number of demands on managers. As firms try to streamline their organizations, the traditional internal boundaries are crumbling and long-accepted practices of workplace organization are challenged.

This study of six prominent American corporations spotlights the demands being made on financial executives and the changing patterns in corporate financial work. As far as we can tell, it is not clear whether the changes in the business environment have penetrated the financial organizations of most companies.

From a research perspective, several questions need to be answered. For instance, is less bureaucracy equated with less control? Or, does less bureaucracy imply more control, in the form of financial responsibility distributed to managers throughout the organization? If the changes occurring in our six firms are an indication, bureaucratic or functionally-oriented controls are being replaced with integrated systems controls in many cases. At the same time, management is participating more in the control process.

Instead of imposing financial controls over other managers, financial executives are being asked to provide more financial leadership. There is an increasing need for financial executives to help form and implement competitive strategy at the business unit level, as well as at the corporate level. Financial executives are doing more with less. As they participate more in business strategy, administrative overhead is being reduced and technology is replacing head count in administrative functions.

Corporate financial organizations are becoming more sophisticated and more productive. However, this is not the entire story. As American firms look to their Asian and European competitors to learn about more effective management practices, they are finding that traditional patterns of financial work cannot go unchallenged.

Recent evidence indicates that Japanese manufacturing firms employ only one-third the number of accountants per direct laborer that American manufacturing firms do (Dixon et al., 1990). The reasons for this disparity are not completely understood. But it is not simply that the Japanese have more quickly realized the benefits of automating the accounting functions. Rather, this disparity stems from profoundly different patterns of administrative work and philosophies of financial control in Japanese and American firms.

For instance, American firms follow more standardized financial practices than their Japanese counterparts, according to a study of business strategy and organization by Kagono et al., (1985). Furthermore, in the U.S. the financial organization has greater influence in decision-making than in Japan. In U.S. firms, the financial organization occupies the second most influential position within the firm. In Japanese firms, the financial organization is the fifth (out of seven) most influential. In view of the success attributed to Japanese management styles and workplace organization, American firms must question all traditional patterns of corporate financial work (as demonstrated in the Ford case study).

This difference in the influence and status of the corporate financial organization lends some empirical plausibility to the argument made by those who claim that the decline of American competitiveness can be traced directly to a management operating philosophy that applies a narrow financial perspective to the formulation and management of competitive strategy. Hayes and Abernathy, in a widely discussed article in the *Harvard Business Review* (1980), are particularly critical of current financial practices. They argue that arm's-length control and detached financial analysis promise sophisticated strategic planning and comprehensive financial control. However, sophisticated analysis and comprehensive control cannot replace the intuition gained from hands-on industrial experience. When managers fail to balance knowledge of the business with analytic sophistication, and when they rely almost totally on the numbers, they undercut their commitment to the innovation in product and process that is essential to long-term competitive success.

While all the blame for competitive decline cannot be placed on American management practices, critics believe that changes in the traditional practices will be a step in the right direction. "Organizational patterns and [management] attitudes" are at the root of the problem of industrial decline, according to Dertouzos et al., (*Made in America: Regaining the Productive Edge*, 1989).

From our literature review, and before conducting our initial interviews at Merck, it appeared that financial executives were being asked to do more with less resources, and equally, if not more important, to do things differently as well.

The key changes in the financial environment and the criticisms we found before conducting the case studies are summarized in the remainder of this chapter.

The Pressures to Change the Financial Organization

As the competitive and regulatory environments of most firms have become more dynamic and complex, the financial implications of all business decisions have become more critical (Gerstner and Anderson, 1976). Even as financial executives are being criticized for contributing to competitive decline, the financial function becomes more critical to the firm's success.

In 1969, the Conference Board conducted its first study of the management of the financial function. Fourteen years later, the Board decided to conduct a second study because of the number of changes that had taken place in the financial environment (Harkins, 1969; Davey, 1983).

The 1983 Conference Board Report cited a number of changes in the financial environment. We have divided the changes into three time periods, covering the last two and one-half decades:

1960s Evolution of the financial control concept. Information explosion. Broad ownership of corporate stock. Government regulation. Growth in trade and consumer credit.

1970s Inflationary spiral, including high and volatile interest rates. Abandonment of fixed exchange rates. Worldwide economic recession. Growth of global markets, including growing competition from low cost, non-Western countries. Rising emphasis on foreign investments and exports. Greater emphasis on internal control, stimulated by public concern over the ethics of corporate managers, especially in dealings with foreign businesses and governments.

1980s Stiffer global competition, resulting in more severe profit pressures. The electronic age, opening the door to more sophisticated financial planning and control, office productivity, and reduced administrative head count. Emerging concern over soaring employee benefit costs. The wave of mergers and acquisitions and the consequent need for both offensive and defensive financial strategies.

With these changes, financial executives need to become key players formulating business strategy. The time has passed when the operating manager decides what will be done and the financial manager finds the funds to do it (Gerstner and Anderson, 1976). This is especially true in the light of global competition. The following quotation supports this view:

> In such a business world, there will be an increasing role for analysis, and the financial officer will be playing from his strength. He will be assessing markets, examining long-term growth rates and market conditions, reviewing exchange rate issues, analyzing local policies relating to protectionism, taxes, currency repatriation, etc. In other words, he will be central to the overall development of a global product strategy . . .

> As part of their involvement in global market strategy, many CFOs are aggressively shaping the future strategy and organization of their companies. According to the interviews we conducted, CEOs are increasingly centralizing corporate strategy in order to get better control over global operations; and in most of the companies we talked to, the financial officer was leading in this effort. (Means, 1987, p.27)

However, changes in the status and scope of the financial function are by no means universal. Nor are they uniform. In the 1983 Conference Board Report (1983), Davey observed a wide variation among firms in the types of changes occurring within the financial organization. He found that of the 255 firms surveyed, nine introduced the position of CFO, while five eliminated the CFO position. Just over one-half of the responding firms reported little or no change in the organization and management of the financial control function, while just under one-half cited some type of change. For instance, the number of respondents who anticipated greater centralization just about equaled the number who expected decentralization.

Some critics feel that it is not necessarily a positive step to require the financial organization to play a greater role in formulating business strategy. They believe that financial executives are contributing to competitive decline and that greater involvement of these executives in forming business strategy will only lead to faster decline. The following section cites some common criticisms that have been directed at the financial organization.

The Managing-by-the-Numbers Debate

These quotations convey the essence of the managing-by-the-numbers debate:

> No business could run without them. Numbers serve as a thermometer that measures the health and well-being of the enterprise. They serve as a first line of communication to inform management what is going on. The more precise the numbers are, the more they are based upon unshakable facts, the clearer the line of communication. (Geneen, 1984, p. 80)

> We manage by the numbers, we judge by the numbers—and we lose by the numbers. (Cohen, quoted in *Business Week,* June 6, 1988, p. 103–4)

> Poor performing companies often have strong cultures, too, but dysfunctional ones. They are usually focused on internal politics rather than on the customer, or they focus on "the numbers" rather than on the product and the people who make and sell it. (Peters and Waterman, 1982, p.76)

> The renewing companies treat facts as friends and financial controls as liberating . . . They have a voracious appetite for facts. Meanwhile, the renewers maintain tight, accurate financial controls. Their people don't regard controls as an imposition of autocracy, but as the benign checks and balances that allow them to be creative and free. (Waterman, 1988)

The most significant problem for CFOs is creating simultaneous loose-tight controls, providing operational autonomy to encourage entrepreneurship, while at the same time adequately controlling the firm's resources. (Vandenburg, quoted in Fleming, 1986, p. 2)

Today's CFO can't afford to just operate by the numbers. He must be down in the trenches where the action is. (McCartney, quoted in Fleming, 1986, p. 28)

As they search for causes of the declining competitiveness of American industry, analysts have been re-examining the effectiveness of all American management practices. Among other things, they question the taken-for-granted assumptions underlying traditional financial management practices. And critics question the manner and degree to which firms should be managed by the numbers. In this study, the debate over the success of managing-by-the-numbers gives us an opportunity to look at the changing character and cost of financial work.

The foregoing quotes trace the evolution of management-by-the-numbers as it has swung, in pendulum fashion, between two extreme positions. In the first quote, Harold Geneen, former ITT Chairman, presents the case for managing-by-the-numbers. He argues that well-managed companies pay close attention to the numbers because the numbers represent the facts of the business.

Cohen, like Hayes and Abernathy (1980), deplores the narrowness of traditional bean-counter approaches to capital budgeting, in which return-on-investment calculations "seek to recover funds only from savings, not from gains in business." In the full article, Cohen claims that narrow approaches to financial justification of investment decisions fail to marry a financial perspective with a sound understanding of the business. Likewise, Peters and Waterman stake out the polar extremes of the management-by-the-numbers debate, which tends to dichotomize management styles based on numbers versus people and products. Financial controls are viewed as part of a dysfunctional, bureaucratic culture.

In their much discussed best-seller *In Search of Excellence,* Peters and Waterman challenged Geneen's philosophy of managing-by-the-numbers and his emphasis on "unshakable facts." Echoing the criticisms raised by Hayes and Abernathy (1980), they disparaged Geneen's philosophy as hard-headed rationality. They argued that it has led to a situation in which "top managers and their staff have become isolated in their analytic ivory towers," thus dangerously distancing themselves from products, customers, and employees. The firm and its employees are treated as financial commodities to be bought and sold in the construction of an optimal portfolio. Managers lose sight of the fact that financial success over the long run is achieved by people and value-adding technology, plus constant attention to product quality and customer service. In a similar fashion, Reich (1983) and others argue that American managers have succumbed to a socially destructive strategy of paper entrepreneurialism.

In criticizing management-by-the-numbers, Peters and Waterman are careful to point out that they are not against quantitative analysis per se. They maintain that America's excellent companies are among the best at getting the numbers, analyzing them, and solving problems. What they object to is a preoccupation with the numbers as a primary means of management. They argue that product-driven and customer-driven styles of management should predominate. Management-by-the-numbers should run a distant second. They suggest that the more successful firms strike an appropriate balance in the manner and degree to which they rely on the numbers.

The last three quotes allude to a middle range position of tensions and trade-offs that must be managed in promoting flexibility and instilling financial discipline in the decision-making process. What these quotes do not address is the nature of financial work itself. And we find virtually no discussion of this matter elsewhere. We would like to find out whether distinct patterns of investment in—and organization of—financial work exist in firms that are more or less numbers-oriented.

A Chance to Examine the Character and Cost of Financial Work

Our research study was designed to probe more deeply into these issues. For instance, what does McCartney mean in saying that the CFO cannot simply operate by the numbers, but must have direct involvement in the day-to-day operations of the various business functions? Just what does "down in the trenches" mean? Does this represent a change in the management philosophy of the CFO and mode of operation of the financial organization? Does this attempt to reduce the distance between people, products, and numbers represent a broader change that cuts across typical American firms?

With the increasing pressure to reduce administrative overhead, what is the appropriate level of investment in the financial function? What changes in management practices must accompany a change in orientation in managing-by-the-numbers? To what extent does the level of investment in financial work depend on the firm's business environment, management's operating philosophy, its unique history, and its traditions?

In Chapter 3, we present evidence of the changes taking place in the character, cost, and orientation of financial work. Then, in Chapter 4 we present a conceptual model of the financial function within a broader context of the organization. We believe the conceptual model will help to identify the changes occurring in the financial organizations of six of America's most prominent firms. We have developed and refined this conceptual model during our talks with the six companies in the case study.

3

Corporate Financial Work:
The Fact of Change in Character,
Cost, and Orientation

One objective of this study was to find out if global competition, government regulation, and technology were having a real impact on financial work in American corporations. Accordingly, we developed a list of topics to be discussed in interviews with senior financial executives in highly respected, major U.S. corporations. The topics were designed to identify any changes that were occurring in the financial organizations of these corporations. This is the list of topics we asked all interviewees to discuss:

1. The critical success factors affecting the financial organization.

2. Changes in the business environment, organization of the workplace, people and events, and measurement practices that had a direct impact on the financial function.

3. The most significant changes that have occurred within the financial organization over the past five to ten years and the implications these changes have on resources available for the financial function.

4. Any special programs or attempts to change the culture within the financial function that have been introduced by the CFO or other senior financial executives to increase the quality of services.

5. The relationship of the financial organization or its members to the operating or business units.

The interviews were conducted in two waves, with three firms participating in each wave. The first three interviews were conducted at Merck, Ford, and AT&T. The second three at 3M, Boeing, and Citicorp.

During the first wave of interviews, we could see that the financial executives in each firm were involved in important changes in the operating philosophy of corporate management. Any concerns that we had that the financial function might be immune to broader changes in the business environment were quickly dispelled at Merck, Ford, and AT&T.

During the second wave of interviews, we found evidence of moderate change at 3M and Boeing, and more radical change at Citicorp. The most dramatic changes in culture and in management philosophy were occurring where the most dramatic changes were taking place in the business environment. However, absence of dramatic change does not mean that the financial organization is out of step with the times. At 3M, the financial organization has a history of continual response to the changing needs of the business units. The firm's approach to financial control goes all the way back to the management philosophy of the first CEO, William McKnight.

Before we describe the nature of the changes at each firm, it might be helpful to point out basic similarities and differences in how each of the financial functions are organized.

Reporting Relationships: We find decentralized financial functions at AT&T, Boeing, Citicorp and Ford. Controllers report on a solid line to the business units and on a dotted line to the corporate financial organization. Merck and 3M have centralized financial functions. The solid line relationship is to the corporate financial organization.

Physical Location of Financial Function Personnel: In AT&T, Boeing, Citicorp, Ford, and Merck the controllers are located with the business units. In 3M, the controllers are centrally located with the corporate financial organization.

Systems Administration and Transactions Processing: All six firms have centralized their financial control system responsibilities. Citicorp, Merck, and 3M have fully integrated systems that allow these financial organizations to prepare financial information on a legal entity, and market or product-line basis from the same database. AT&T, Boeing, and Ford are not as far along in fully integrating their financial systems.

The current organization of the financial function may reflect a recent change in management operating philosophy, as at AT&T. Or it may reflect a commitment that has not changed over fifty years, as at 3M.

At this point we want to lay out the basic facts of change at each of the six corporations. This will provide a foundation on which to base the conceptual model that will be developed in Chapter 4. This conceptual model will be used in telling the story of the individual case studies in Section B of this monograph.

In Table 1 we have identified themes and trends in the management of the financial function across all six firms. We have identified:

1. Key economic factors that have had an impact on the financial function.

2. Aspects of the firm's history, strategy, and structure that have influenced the financial function.

3. Shifts within the function that are tied to the management strategies for bringing about change.

Table 1 profiles six distinct stories of change in the management of the financial function. On the surface it would appear that the executives of each financial function are preoccupied with a uniquely different set of issues in response to firm-specific conditions. Yet, there is a deeper pattern that connects the changes occurring in each financial function. In the next chapter and the individual cases presented in Section 2, we will discuss the nature of that pattern. But first, we elaborate on some of the themes and trends summarized in Table 1.

Themes and Trends

The following paragraphs elaborate on some of these themes and trends firm-by-firm.

Merck

The story of change at Merck can be summed up in one word: sophistication. Today, the members of the financial organization are considered to be highly qualified financial professionals. They are full members of the management teams at both the business-unit level and the corporate level. The company has made major investments to upgrade the analytic sophistication of the financial organization that are needed to give value-added support services to the line operations.

Under the leadership and vision of the current CFO, Merck's financial professionals are expected to engage in financial R&D activities. The financial organization is expected to play a leadership role in developing financial tools to support research, manufacturing, and marketing. Financial professionals have come to be valued as important and integral mem-

TABLE 1   Themes and Trends in the Management of the Financial Function

	Merck	Ford
Key Economic Factors	Intensified product competition from foreign and generic drug competitors	Intense price and product competition
	Potentially more restrictive/unfavorable regulatory environment	High strategic risk of new car development and global product strategy
	High strategic risk of ethical R&D	
Firm History, Strategy, Structure	Unique background and orientation of current CEO	Functional (chimney) orientation of firm
	Major contribution by financial function to financial resurgence of Merck	Historical power of finance staff
		The Mazda benchmark studies
Shifts and Strategies in Financial Function Management	Major effort to upgrade sophistication of financial analysis and professionalism of financial staff	Shift in orientation from command/control to competitive-team
	Program of institutional research and advocacy designed to influence regulatory environment	Philosophy of continuous improvement coupled with program of process simplification and system commonization
	Leading edge culture of innovation in financial tools and products	Reallocation of analytic effort from downstream to upstream strategic analysis
		Upgrade of product cost information
		Significant downsizing of financial staff

bers of their management teams. In a firm that has been voted America's most admired corporation for the last three years in *Fortune Magazine*'s annual survey of corporate executives, the financial organization has been consistently rated as the top staff function.

Ford

The story of change in Ford's financial function over the past ten years is one of major improvements in efficiency, combined with increasing emphasis on financial support for the business operations. Responding to a competitive crisis, Ford initiated a basic cultural shift from a strong, functionally oriented, chain-of-command management style to a more team-oriented, integrated management style. The finance staff has had to change from being after-the-fact, second-guessing, goal tenders, to being team players.

TABLE 1 *Continued*

	AT&T	3M
Key Economic Factors	Upon divestiture, entry into competitive market characterized by severe price and product competition	Change in organization for global competition
	The only regulated player in an unregulated market	Integration of international business
	High strategic risk associated with rapidly changing technology and competition for megadeals	Integration of taxes with business operations
		Committment to increase government business
Firm History, Strategy, Structure	Historically functional orientation and structure of firm	Strong influence of first CEO for a centralized financial function and decentralized businesses
	Institutionalized staff mentality of regulatory conformance	Headcount control creates a tension between efficiency and customer service
	Organizational tension created by information management and movement market	Current CEO orientation to numbers and details
Shifts and Strategies in Financial Function Management	Shift in orientation from conformance to competitive team with related effort to upgrade quality of financial information and analysis	Refocus on a full set of financial targets to measure success
	Commonization and consolidation of highly fragmented pre-divestiture financial systems	Concern about the balance between technical/interpersonal skills of financial function professionals
	Upgrade of product costing methodology and information	Concern about the over analysis/ more analysis tension
	Significant downsizing of financial staff	

This shift has changed the character of financial work at Ford. First, financial analysis places less emphasis on downstream monitoring of operations and gives more attention to upstream competitive analysis. Second, by shifting emphasis away from corporate oversight and placing responsibility for cost control within the team, the financial organization has concentrated on simplifying and streamlining its transaction-processing and control systems. Simplification has greatly reduced redundant administrative work. This change in management philosophy has contributed much to efficiency. Ford has been able to reduce the personnel in the financial function by more than 40 percent since 1979.

TABLE 1 *Continued*

	Citicorp	Boeing
Key Economic Factors	Need for an orthodox financial control function to cope with more complex financial markets FASB impact on Citicorp's customers and need for strategic risk assessment	Global price/product competition on commercial side Strategic risk of government compliance violations on military side
Firm History, Strategy, Structure	Strong CEO emphasis on numbers control, informal structure Creation of a financial control function from scratch Dedication to extreme decentralization and business integration Emphasis on individual contributions from professional staff	Higher financial function cost of military business due to management philosophy and organizational strategy Production/Cost control tension due to massive backlog on commercial side Financial/Management information not integrated on commercial side Commercial/Military differences pervasive
Shifts and Strategies in Financial Function Management	Emphasis on the financial function versus the function per se Heavy commitment to financial engineering and accounting risk analysis Increased participation on external committees that affect Citicorp success	Beefed-up internal audit function to insure government compliance Move to standardized financial accounting systems in response to management dissatisfaction Some movement to design-to-cost teams

AT&T

Changes at AT&T stem directly from its transition from a regulated monopoly to a global competitor. The full impact of this transition on AT&T's financial organization has not yet been realized. Basically, the shift from total regulation to selective regulation and global competition is placing multiple demands on the financial organization. In the past, the financial people were concerned mainly with technical compliance with externally imposed rules and procedures of regulatory agencies. However, in December 1983 (date of divestiture), AT&T found itself short of people with sophisticated financial analysis skills, leadership abilities, and a penchant to work close to the business.

As at Citicorp, AT&T's financial executives face the challenge of creating a culture of financial professionals and financial managers out of a culture of green-eyeshade accountants. This is difficult when most of the employees in the financial organization have never been expected to play a major role in decision-making. Earning the right to sit at the decision-making table is a key objective of AT&T's senior financial executives. It's not easy, because knowledge of the business must be learned through experience, whereas the rules and regulations they have previously followed have been established by edict.

AT&T's senior financial executives are now pushing their financial people closer to the businesses. Of all the firms included in the study, this company is the most deeply involved in significant changes in all areas of its financial function.

3M

At 3M, the change is not as obvious as at Ford, Merck, Citicorp, and AT&T. With their existing accounting system, their financial organization can generate more than 3500 P&L statements a month. This system allows them to respond to important changes in the business environment without making any major changes in management operating philosophy or organization of the workplace.

No dramatic shifts in orientation have been caused at 3M by competitive crisis, divestiture, or deregulation. What we do observe in this case is how a financial organization can respond to change if it has a fundamentally sound and integrated financial accounting system. As with each of the other firms in this study, the increasing scope and complexity of global competition requires 3M to engage in more sophisticated financial analysis. Its financial executives realize that they must upgrade the sophistication of the financial professionals who are assigned to the business units.

3M has a strong, independent, highly centralized financial organization, subject to corporate head count control. As such, the financial organization has to maintain a balance between service to the client and administrative efficiency—between being involved and being independent.

Citicorp

In Citicorp's financial organization, we find dramatic change in response to deregulation and diversification. The company's financial executives talk about building the current financial control function from ground zero. Over the last decade and a half, the corporate financial organization has been transformed from a group of green-eye-shade accountants to highly sophisticated financial professionals. They take pride in being integral members of their management teams. The conversion is due largely to the support of the current CEO, John Reed, and the former CEO, Walter Wriston. In the past, financial control meant knowing the manuals. Today, financial control means knowing the business and managing risks.

Boeing

Changes are occurring throughout Boeing, but in different ways, depending on where one is in the organization. Because of the difference between Boeing's military and commercial businesses, its financial organization has a less unified culture than found at the other five firms. As a result, we find three stories in one when we look at Boeing's financial function. First, the orientation of the corporate financial function differs from that of the business-unit functions. Second, there are clear differences in the nature and organization of financial groups between the commercial and military sides of the firm.

Some of the singular changes in the financial function at Boeing are being driven from the bottom-up—from the divisions up to corporate level. These changes are being triggered by an increasingly competitive environment on both the commercial and military sides of the business. The changes at the corporate financial level seem to be directly related to the historically strong oversight orientation.

Within the military business-unit functions, change is easier to define and identify. Because military contracting is competitive, Boeing has developed a strong program-oriented and project-oriented management philosophy that pushes financial control responsibility down into the organization. At the same time, at the corporate level, the internal auditing group is being beefed-up to minimize the risk of government contract violations.

On the commercial side of Boeing, new design-to-cost and design-to-build philosophies are being implemented to help Boeing reduce cost.

Finding Patterns of Variation and Change

In this chapter, we have briefly described the changes taking place in each of the six firms. But we need to go beyond mere documentation if we are to gain a research perspective and if we want to anticipate the needs of financial executives contemplating changes in their organizations.

We believe that before financial executives make dramatic changes, they must be aware of their firm's business environment, the values of its work-place and its history and culture. They need to take a long, hard look at the entire financial function. This is indicated by the three basic orientations to financial work that we have identified in this study. Piece-meal change is not likely to work.

In Chapter 4, we present the conceptual model which emerged from our research. Here we see how all the elements under a specific orientation must be considered together in bringing about change.

4

Understanding Patterns of Variation and Change in Financial Management

To fully appreciate the broad patterns of change taking place in financial organizations of American corporations, we believe it is important to understand the concept of orientation of financial functions.

We have identified these three distinct orientations to financial work:

1. Command-and-control

2. Conformance

3. Competitive-team

Each of the firms in this study falls into one of these distinct orientations to financial work, or falls between two of the orientations. Likewise, the changes taking place in each firm are understood in terms of involvement from one orientation to another.

Each orientation follows a distinct pattern of involvement of the financial organization in the management of the firm. The character and costs associated with the financial function vary with each orientation. A financial organization with a competitive-team orientation makes a different type of contribution to the success of the firm than a financial organization with a command-and-control orientation or one with a conformance orientation.

In the Executive Summary we introduced Figure 1, which shows the three orientations for the financial function as interlocking circles. All corporate financial organizations must deal with corporate hierarchy, rules and regulations, and product and financial markets. Yet, we have found that one of the three orientations seems to predominate in any firm.

The concept of orientation of financial function was not specifically mentioned by the executives during our interviews. Rather, in firms experiencing the most change, financial executives talked about changing their culture or reorienting the financial function to meet the challenges of global competition or changes in government regulation. They frequently articulated their vision of the function as changing to match the changing business conditions. A new orientation was being contrasted to an old orientation.

In several cases, most notably Ford, AT&T and Citicorp, this reorientation called for a total rethinking of how the financial organization contributes to the success of the firm. As we contrasted the old and new in the interview data, the concept of the three distinct orientations emerged.

The Evolution of a Conceptual Model

The Ford and AT&T interviews were particularly eventful. Financial executives at these firms constantly referred to the organizational culture within their firms. Without a doubt, the corporate culture had a tremendous impact on the character and costs of corporate financial work. Virtually every person interviewed in each of these firms emphasized the reorientation that the financial organization was undergoing as part of a larger change in corporate culture. The cultural shift going on within each firm was having had a dramatic, even revolutionary, effect on every aspect of financial work. Ford and AT&T were changing their financial organizations in very different ways. Yet, the direction in which each was moving allowed us to construct the three basic orientations to financial work.

By the end of the last set of interviews, we found that the three orientations provided a useful way to explain patterns of variation and change in all six organizations. For example, at Ford they talked about replacing a top-down, command-and-control management style with a much more team-oriented style. This shift to a team orientation, with a focus on beating the competition, has altered the pattern of financial work at Ford.

In the early 1980s, there was a consensus at Ford that some type of drastic measures had to be taken to emerge from their economic crisis. The reorientation of the financial function was just one part of a major change in organizational strategy and culture. The reorientation within the financial function was accelerated by what Ford learned during detailed studies of Mazda's style of management. Ford began to realize that many of its accounting and control practices were heavily influenced by a command-and-control management style. Financial controls were much different in the Mazda culture. If for no reason other than straight cost reduction, Ford began to modify its approach to control and the patterns of financial work.

The financial executives at AT&T talked about the need to get ready for competition by replacing a highly functional and bureaucratic mind-set with a market-oriented mind-set. It became clear that AT&T's financial organization was driven by a history of being a regulated domestic monopoly oriented to conforming to federal, state, and local regulations. In this context, the financial organization, outside of the treasury function, was very much of a bookkeeping function designed to demonstrate technical compliance with externally imposed rules.

AT&T realized that this conformance mind-set was totally inadequate to meet the financial information needs of managers in the deregulated, competitive environment after divestiture. Managers now needed to know the true costs, the real economics of doing business in a competitive environment. The financial systems could not meet the needs of the new AT&T. And the people were not trained to think in terms of the type of information required to support the formulation and management of competitive business strategy.

From the Ford and AT&T interviews, we could see that about the only thing the two organizations had in common was the fact that each organization was responsible for similar basic financial management tasks. Also, each financial organization was evolving—moving away from a dominant orientation to financial work. Their starting points were different, but both companies were converging on the same new orientation.

In Ford's case there were two distinct orientations. The one in effect before the competitive crisis we have labelled command-and-control. The one that emerged after the competitive crisis we call the competitive-team orientation. There were also two distinct orientations in the AT&T interviews. Before divestiture, they were in a conformance orientation. After divestiture, they entered a competitive-team orientation. In the two firms we found three distinct orientations—command-and-control, conformance, and competitive-team.

As our study proceeded, we found that these three orientations helped capture the nature of the changes taking place at the other four firms. Our analysis of these firms helped to flesh out the different dimensions of each orientation and the different ways an orientation is embodied from firm to firm.

While identifying the three orientations to financial work, we focused on the dynamics of change. However, the broader organizational context cannot be ignored when talking about orientations. Figure 2 embeds the three orientations to financial work within a broader organizational context. It consists of the business environment, workplace organization, people and events, and measurement practices.

The four components of organizational context have had a dramatic effect on the current status of the financial organization within each firm.

The stories of the six financial organizations can be told using Figure 2 as a common background. Yet, each case study offers a unique story in its own right. The conceptual model, which we believe will be of interest to other financial executives, emerged from the six concrete case histories. It would not exist in its present form without them.

The Conceptual Model

The conceptual model shown in Figure 2 sets forth the relationships among:

☐ The business environment

☐ Work place organization

☐ People and events

☐ Measurement practices

The components in the corners of the model interact to create the conditions for one of the three orientations to emerge as dominant in a particular firm. The three orientations are depicted as the three interlocking circles of the triangle. Each orientation entails a different pattern in the character and costs of corporate financial work. Within each orientation, a different mix of financial services is emphasized, different control relationships are maintained, and the way executives talk about people, training and development, and leadership vary dramatically.

FIGURE 2 Components of Organizational Context

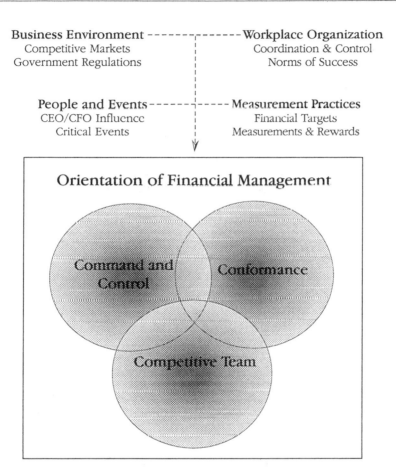

Business Environment ------- ------- Workplace Organization
Competitive Markets   Coordination & Control
Government Regulations   Norms of Success

People and Events ------ ----- Measurement Practices
CEO/CFO Influence   Financial Targets
Critical Events   Measurements & Rewards

Orientation of Financial Management

Command and Control

Conformance

Competitive Team

A financial organization that is pulled closer to a command-and-control orientation will differ in systematic ways from a financial organization that is pulled toward a competitive-team or conformance orientation. More than one orientation can emerge within the same firm as with 3M and Boeing. For example, in the 3M case, the business units represent the epitome of a competitive-team orientation. The corporate staff units, on the other hand, are primarily of a command-and-control orientation. The financial organization at 3M has adapted this dual orientation in order to meet the needs of both the business and corporate units.

Before we concentrate on the elements making up each financial function orientation, we will discuss the four corners of the model—the components of organizational context.

The Business Environment

The business environment has two subdivisions—competitive markets and government regulation. Under competitive markets, the financial executives discussed issues related to global business strategy, the effects of competition, and the impact of doing business with the government. Under government regulation, executives focused on the costs of complying with regulations and the strategic uncertainties and risks associated with possible contract violations and sudden changes in statutory requirements. Citicorp in particular emphasized the costs of regulation and risks associated with FASB activities.

AT&T and Boeing were asked to participate in the study specifically because of the amount of business they do with the government or because of the effects of divestiture and deregulation. However, to a surprisingly large extent, all six financial organizations were directly affected by government involvement in the economy.

A concept that we have not developed up to this point but that we feel captures a key impact of the business environment on the orientation and involvement of the financial function is strategic risk. There is greater risk associated with strategic thrusts that 1) expose the firm to significant loss of resources, even to the point of threatening business viability, and 2) are difficult to predict because of highly complex and dynamic technological and market forces. Strategic risk is typically a function of highly interdependent relationships within the business.

High strategic risk tends to increase the involvement of the financial function in the formulation and management of competitive strategy. Such financial analysis adds value to the strategic decision process by enabling a full and complete assessment of the competitive and regulatory dimensions of a hostile environment, thereby providing a basis for contingency planning that improves the firm's ability to adapt to changing conditions. Thus, the main impact of increasing strategic risk is to increase the comprehensiveness and sophistication of the financially-based competitive analysis that demanded by top and divisional management, and thereby, to increase the upstream involvement of financial staff in the strategic management of the business.

As the case studies in Section B document, each of the firms in this study has experienced an increase in strategic risk associated with heightened competitive intensity, shortened product lifecycles, implementation of global product strategies involving substantial investment of resources, and deregulation. Thus, the involvement of the financial organization in the strategic management of business has increased most in the firms that have experienced the greatest amount of change in strategic risk.

However, greater strategic risk does not necessarily lead to the competitive team orientation. It can just as well lead to a strong command and control orientation. Ford and Boeing are good examples in this regard. Both firms have always had (or their management have historically operated under the premise of) high strategic risk. Historically these two firms have had strong command and control orientations. Thus, the other factors depicted in Figure 2 play an equally important role in combining with the uncertainty of the competitive and regulatory environment to influence the orientation of the financial function.

Workplace Organization

The work-place organization also has two subdivisions—coordination and control, and norms of success. Under coordination and control, executives talked about centralization and decentralization, and relationships between corporate and business units. They also discussed differentiation by customer, by market, and by country, as well as creating a matrix relationship between finance and the business units. Major changes have occurred at Ford, Citicorp, and AT&T in management philosophy regarding the best way to coordinate and control operations through financial information and financial services. At Boeing, Merck and 3M, few, if any, changes are being made in issues of coordination and control.

Interestingly though, seemingly similar philosophies of coordination and control can result in different financial function orientations. A comparison of Citicorp and 3M is instructive in this regard. Both firms have highly entreprenurial operating philosophies and decentralized management structures. Yet, as the cases of these two firms bring out, Citicorp has a much stronger competitive team orientation than does 3M. The reason for this difference is not explained by philosophies of coordination and control, but rather by other differences between the firms, not the least of which is the long standing system of centralized financial control established by 3M's first CEO.

Under norms of success, executives pointed to organizational expectations, contributions of individuals, bases of legitimacy and credibility, and communication patterns that influence the orientation of the financial function. For example, under organizational expectations, Ford placed the most emphasis on continuous process improvement. Merck stressed being on the leading-edge of research and development, both for the firm as a whole and within the financial function. 3M accented efficiency and customer service. The executives at Merck and Citicorp stressed the importance of making personal, individual, value-added contributions to the success of the firm. They also mentioned how important training and development are, and how legitimacy is based on individual expertise and is critical in establishing a professional financial function.

Overall, the executives at Ford, Merck, and Citicorp devoted considerably more time to issues related to the workplace organization—in particular the norms of success—than the executives at the other three firms.

People and Events

Under people and events, the subdivisions are CEO/CFO influence and critical events. With our interview-based method, we were able to identify very concrete and particular influences on the orientation of the financial function that would have been impossible with a survey approach. At Ford, Merck, Citicorp, and 3M, people we interviewed stressed the tremendous impact that the CEO and CFO have on the orientation of the financial function. For example, the financial organizations at Merck and Citicorp might look entirely different under different CEO and/or CFO leadership. At Citicorp, the leadership of CEO John Reed and Executive Vice President Tom Jones has been very evident, likewise, at Merck, CEO Roy Vagelos and CFO Frank Spiegel have exerted a strong personal influence on the financial function. The history of the financial organization at Ford is closely associated with the wiz kids, including a former CFO, Edward Lundy. The financial organization at 3M is talked about in terms of the influence of the first CEO, William McKnight, who started his career with 3M as a bookkeeper.

The Ford and AT&T cases stress the role that critical events play in changing the orientation of a financial function. In Ford we have the economic crisis of the early 1980s, which affected the entire firm. We also have the detailed Mazda studies, which showed Ford a different way of maintaining financial control at considerably less cost. The AT&T and Citicorp stories document the changes that are occurring in the financial function as a direct result of divestiture and/or deregulation. AT&T is undergoing the most dramatic changes in all aspects of financial organization as a result of the court decision to split up Ma Bell.

Measurement Practices

The two components of measurement practices are measurement and reward. Merck, Citicorp, and 3M stress how important profitability targets are to top management in measuring performance. Boeing underscores the importance of cost targets. Ford intervieweesdid not emphasize financial targets during the interviews. In Ford's case, part of the shift in orientation of the financial function may have been precipitated by a notion that too much attention was being paid to the numbers. At the time of our interviews at AT&T, measurement and reward practices were undergoing continual modification as management searched for the best "market facing" organized structure and a management process that promoted entrepreneurial behavior within a framework of corporate-wide goals. Top financial executives were heavily involved in this process. Also, AT&T was in negotiating to change from rate-of-return regulation to price-cap regulation. The firm's executives were reluctant to speak at length about the possible outcome.

While the competitive crisis created the mandate for change, Ford's detailed studies of Mazda helped management to see the nature and extent of change required in engineering, production, and financial control practices. As the Ford case documents, the Mazda studies showed Ford's financial executives how a different, more team oriented operating philosophy could lead to a different way of maintaining financial control at considerably less cost.

On the importance of financial measurement, Merck, Citicorp, and 3M talked about their integrated financial systems, which provide legal entity and product/market information from the same database. They also explained how their systems are tied directly to the management performance evaluation and reward system. At the time of the interviews, Ford, AT&T, and Boeing did not have financial systems comparable to the other three.

TABLE 2 Orientations to Corporate Financial Work

	Competitive-Team	Command-and-Control	Conformance
Context			
Focal Environment	Market	Corporate	Regulatory
Style of Workplace Organization	Matrix Integrative	Functional Chain of command	Bureaucratic Fixed routines
Financial Organization Norms			
Predominant Mind-set of Financial Function	Leadership/ Service	Oversight	External accountability
Criterion of Success	Value-added involvement	Operating efficiency	Technical compliance
Primary Role of Financial Person	Financial professional/ manager	Controller/ cost accountant	Bookkeeper/ administrator
Primary Source of Status/Legitimacy	Business judgement and financial expertise	Position in hierarchy as steward of corporate resources Independent third party	Technical knowledge of rules Custodian of accounts
Character and Cost of Services			
Analysis: *Character*	*Strategic Upstream Sophisticated	Internal monitoring Downstream	Minimal Oriented to external advocacy
Cost	*High	Medium	Low
Control: *Character*	Checks and balances maintained collectively by business team	*Power of the veto Arm's-length relationship	Technical compliance with external standards
Cost	Low	*High	Medium
Accounting: *Character*	Streamlined Product oriented	Elaborate Control laden	*Elaborate Externally driven
Cost	Low	High	*High

* Dominant service

The Combined Effects

When viewed within the context of Figure 2, no two of the six firms have similar histories or cultures. In fact, the uniqueness of each firm, along with its importance and prominence in corporate America, was one of the criteria used for inclusion in the study. Yet, even with the differences, we have found similar patterns of variation and change within the financial organizations of all six. The three orientations are meant to capture these similarities.

The Orientations to Financial Work

Table 2 presents the essential features of the three orientations to financial work. Each orientation is linked to the broader organization context by reference to:

☐ A focal environment and style of workplace organization.

☐ A set of financial organization norms.

☐ The character and cost of financial function services.

We'll discuss the elements falling within each orientation in terms of context, norms and character, and cost of services.

The Command-and-Control Orientation

Context The command-and-control orientation to financial work draws strong authority from the corporate management hierarchy. The firm as a whole is organized on a functional basis, with the functional organization carrying over to the financial function itself. For example, distinctions are maintained between controllership and treasury, etc. Communication flows up and down the chain of command, with little horizontal communication at the lower levels of the organization. Under a command-and-control orientation, the primary financial management challenge is to maintain internal control over the resources owned by the corporation.

Financial Organization Norms The financial organization is responsible for overseeing the use of corporate resources. It prepares an independent review of the financial aspects of business plans prepared by the operating units. The principal criterion of success is operating or administrative efficiency. The financial function oriented toward command-and-control has many people assigned to cost accounting and cost analysis. Stewardship over the physical and financial (versus human) resources provides the authority for the members of the financial function. To be successful, the financial organization must be an independent third party.

Character and Cost of Services Under the command-and-control orientation, analysis is directed toward monitoring the financial performance of all other operating and administrative units within the firm. It tends to concentrate on minute budgetary details.

The financial organization exercises control through the power of the veto. It is considered desirable to maintain an arm's-length relationship to the other operating units. The accounting system is designed to provide financial information that matches the functional organization of the firm. The accounting system needs to be elaborate and control-laden to make it easy to provide oversight and monitor internal performance.

The Argument for Command-and-Control In environments where there is mild competition and significant economies of scale, success stems from the efficient use of resources. Owners and top management have traditionally placed the locus of responsibility for control with the financial organization. Since World War II, growth in domestic demand for goods and services could almost be taken for granted. The management challenge, until the mid-1970s, was to allocate scarce resources to meet growing customer demands with little or no foreign competition. The command-and-control orientation was appropriate during this period. It may still be for firms operating in mildly competitive environments, although there is growing recognition that highly functional organizational structures are neither the most efficient nor most effective.

Furthermore, the recent trend in corporate restructuring, which has increased the debt load of many corporations, is worth noting at this point. Heavy debt loads associated with takeovers and leveraged buyouts are assumed under the new owners' presumption that their firms can be run more efficiently. Thus, these types of restructurings tend to fix managerial attention on issues of cost control and financial asset management. In the absence of any countervailing forces, we suspect that the heavy emphasis on control of corporate resources in highly debt-ladden firms may push the financial function in these firms toward a command and control orientation.

The Conformance Orientation

Context The conformance orientation to financial work focuses on external regulation. The financial function is organized as a bureaucracy. Fixed routines are established to process the accounting information required by regulatory agencies. The flow of communication is designed mainly to provide clarifications, for regulatory purposes, of data submitted in accounting documents.

Financial Organization Norms Members of the financial organization are primarily concerned with external accountability, established through legislation or administrative procedures. Success is based on technical compliance with the rules. The typical financial person is the bookkeeper-type accountant. The status of the financial organization is based on detailed knowledge of the technical and procedural rules that must be followed to obey the law. The financial organization is regarded as the custodian of accounts or the keeper of the books.

Character and Cost of Services There is minimal need for analysis under the conformance orientation. Whatever analysis does take place is to support external advocacy objectives, such as to justify rate increases before regulatory commissions. Control is strictly interpreted as technical compliance with external rules and standards. The accounting system is driven by external reporting and accountability requirements.

The Argument for Conformance When the public interest is at stake, as in maintaining a domestic telecommunications system, a fixed, bureaucratic financial control system is thought desirable to protect the public and to minimize the chances of major financial failure. The same is true when competitive markets are considered inappropriate for regulating performance, as in the banking industry of the recent past, or possibly the savings and loan industry of today. National and local monopolies are closely monitored to insure accountability. The public is protected from exploitation by large corporations, while the large corporations are protected from the perils of the market through a system of regulated prices.

In a regulatory environment, the demand for change is weak. The movement away from highly regulated businesses and industries has been the single most important reason behind the current movement away from the conformance orientation.

The Competitive-Team Orientation

Context The competitive-team orientation to financial work is focused primarily on external competitive markets, although the financial organization also has its internal customers. The firm as a whole is managed along matrix organizational lines, with strong emphasis placed on integration versus functional specialization or bureaucratic routine. Communication flows horizontally. People rely heavily on informal communication. All members of the management team need to know the financial implications of their decisions. The financial organization has dual responsibilities and dual accountabilities. Its responsibility is to support business units and, at the same time, maintain the integrity of the corporate financial system.

Financial Organization Norms Financial executives think mainly of getting close to the business, servicing the business units and corporate customer, and providing financial leadership in forming business strategy. The major criterion for success is valued-added involvement through demonstrated performance in adding to the bottom line.

Members of the financial organization are first and foremost considered to be financial professionals or financial managers, rather than cost accountants or bookkeepers. Issues of operating efficiency and technical compliance are subsumed under a more broadly defined value-added guideline for success.

Legitimacy within the firm is based on professional expertise, rather than on position in the hierarchy or mere technical knowledge of rules and regulations. Training and development are considered important investments in people who must provide the level of sophisticated services demanded by the business units facing heightened levels of risk and competition.

Character and Cost of Services Under the competitive-team orientation, analysis is tied directly to business strategy. Competitive analysis to support the business teams and financial analysis tied to risk/return concepts are the hallmarks of involvement in the financial function. In organizations that have shifted to the competitive-team orientation, financial analysis has moved upstream to the formulation of business strategy.

Financial control is maintained within the competitive team. The concept of ownership has been pushed down to the team level. Stewardship responsibilities are equated with management responsibilities and are not the sole province of the financial people. Financial professionals are expected to be the conscience of their companies. They also are personally responsible for any breakdown in internal financial controls.

The accounting system is designed to provide product and market information to the business units and legal entity information for external accountability. Financial controls are streamlined and integrated into the basic business operating systems wherever possible. Heavy reliance on sophisticated computer systems reduces the number of people needed to do processing tasks and allows the financial organization to reallocate the human resources to analysis tasks.

The Argument for Competitive-Team The shift to the competitive-team orientation is most appropriate in highly competitive environments. To be a world class competitor, a firm must outperform the competition in terms of price, performance and profitability. Financial sophistication must be dispersed throughout the organization to insure that operating decisions in the business units are financially sound over short and long term.

The joint imperatives for innovation and efficiency require a management philosophy for organizing the workplace that promotes entrepreneurial, as well as financial, discipline. Simply stated, when the basis of success is primarily knowledge of the business, instead of stewardship over corporate resources or knowledge of the rules, the competitive-team orientation seems to have some distinct advantages.

What to Expect From the Case Studies

We gave each of the six firms in this study an opportunity to review their story within the context of the other five stories. In 3M's case, the relative emphasis of the story was revised, resulting in increased attention to 3M's financial systems capabilities. No other material changes were made to the stories as originally written.

Each story is told within the framework of the conceptual model represented in Figures 1 and 2. Rather than apply a single rigid format to each case history, we have tried to preserve the uniqueness of each by following the flow which emerged from the interviews. Aside from specific references to shifts in orientation or position between two orientations, the elements of context, norms of financial organization and character and cost of services have been woven into the each story as these elements emerged from the interviews.

Briefly, the Ford case is a story of shift from a strong command-and-control orientation to a competitive-team orientation. The Merck case is told as a change from muted command-and-control to a competitive-team orientation. The Citicorp story is one of shift from a conformance orientation to a competitive-team orientation. The 3M case is told as a financial organization positioned between command-and-control and competitive-team. The AT&T story is told in terms of its current efforts to move away from a combination of command-and-control and conformance to competitive-team. The Boeing case is told as three short stories. The commercial side of Boeing is making some effort to move toward competitive-team from command-and-control. The military side of Boeing shows slightly more movement from conformance to competitive-team. The corporate organization, on the other hand, is firmly positioned between command-and-control and conformance.

5

Challenge to Education

Summary

We concur with those who are calling for a fundamental reorientation of the business curriculum. We believe our conceptual model of orientations to corporate financial work provides a useful framework for critiquing the current state of business education and, in particular, the accounting curriculum. We hope we can offer a perspective on the need for change in business education.

From the standpoint of professors wishing to interact with students, the emergence of the competitive-team model may provide just the right pressure to give students a more well-rounded education. In addition to course content and structure, the implications of our findings speak directly to the sophistication of those who teach. Professors of accounting and finance, like their corporate counterparts, need to get closer to the business if we are going to educate the type of student some firms in corporate America seem to require.

The Implications of the Research Findings

In Chapter 3, we documented the change in the character, cost and orientation of financial work in the six firms included in this study. And, as summarized in Chapter 1, the changes in the character and cost of financial work can be classified into three broad categories:

☐ Firms are either reallocating existing resources or investing in additional resources to achieve the greater sophistication of financial analysis and financial systems and services needed to support the management of global strategy.

☐   In some firms, the walls between finance and line management are being torn down. Financial control is becoming a shared responsibility for all members of the management team. This shared responsibility is creating a new ethic of financial communication and information sharing. Line managers are now being required to become more financially literate, while financial managers are being required to share information, to communicate, and to become more business literate. Furthermore, financial executives are being asked to accept more responsibility for the achievement of "non-financial" aspects of business performance, such as product quality and customer service.

☐   Firms with financial systems based on elaborate functions or bureaucracy are striving to simplify and streamline their systems to become more product- and customer-oriented. Firms that already have integrated financial systems are reducing their administrative costs by using state-of-the-art computer technology. Resources thus freed are being reallocated to support more sophisticated analysis.

These changes in the character and cost of financial work, along with the emergence of the competitive-team orientation, are but a component of a broader shift in American management practices. In response to global competition, firms are moving toward leaner, more flexible, more knowledge-based forms of corporate organization. Financial executives in all six firms of this study are facing changing management expectations. Individual financial professionals must now get closer to the business, be able to apply a multi-disciplinary perspective to business problems and accept more responsibility for the achievement of corporate financial goals.

In this chapter, we will discuss the implications of our research findings on the business curriculum in American colleges and universities. In the first section, we will present the differences in recruiting strategies among the six firms.

In the second section, we will relate the different recruiting strategies to the findings of a separate FERF study of the development of financial executives, which is scheduled for publication in the summer of 1990. Just as corporate managers are being asked to do more with fewer resources, the financial executives interviewed by The Gallup Organization appear to want new hires to supplement the traditionally strong accounting and analytical skills with increased communication skills and a greater understanding of the business.

In the third section, we will offer a critique of the current undergraduate accounting program within the context of the command-and-control and conformance orientations of our conceptual model. Then we will speculate about a vision of a new financial management university major within the context of the competitive-team orientation.

The critique focuses on the undergraduate accounting major, since accounting is still the predominant discipline that financial executives believe is an essential foundation for success. We urge financial executives from corporate America to take a more positive stance in working with colleges and universities, if they want to have as much influence over the accounting curriculum as the big six public accounting firms.

Recruiting and Development Strategies

The six case studies exhibit patterns of variation and change within the financial function in corporate America. From a research perspective, the conceptual model described in Chapter 4 captures these changes in terms of three basic financial function orientations: command-and-control, conformance, and competitive-team. From the perspective of recruiting strategy, we have also found that firms that have made the greatest commitment to the competitive-team orientation follow a different recruiting strategy than the firms more closely tied to command-and-control and conformance orientations.

Citicorp, Ford, and Merck recruit individuals with an average of six to eight years work experience beyond the bachelor's degree. Candidates for financial professional positions have either an advanced degree, primarily an MBA or a CPA, with six to eight years of public accounting experience. AT&T, Boeing and 3M recruit at the bachelor's degree level. The typical recruit has an undergraduate degree in accounting.

In the three firms that have made the most obvious moves toward the competitive-team orientation—Ford, Merck, and Citicorp—financial professionals are generally recruited from the ranks of the top MBA schools and from the big six public accounting firms. These three are looking for MBAs who can step right into the organization and immediately start making value-added contributions. Typically these individuals have concentrated on finance in their MBA program. The MBAs from the top schools are in demand because of their strong analytic skills and, hopefully, strong communication and interpersonal skills. In the late 1970s and early 1980s, it was often difficult to attract the best MBA talent because of the higher salaries being paid to top students by investment banking institutions. However, in recent years, all three firms have reentered the MBA market at the high end of the salary scale to attract the best talent.

For some corporate financial control positions, Citicorp and Merck also recruit CPAs with six to eight years experience from the large public accounting firms. These two firms, in effect, recruit from a pool of individuals whose talent lies in their strong technical accounting skills. Once these individuals have been hired, Citicorp cross-trains the MBAs and CPAs to get a balance between the analytic skills of the MBAs and technical accounting skills of the CPAs.

Financial professionals at AT&T, Boeing, and 3M have been recruited primarily from the ranks of undergraduate accounting majors. Even though we have characterized AT&T as moving toward the competitive-team orientation, the interviews produced no evidence that the firm was changing its recruiting strategy to go for more MBAs. It is moving key experienced financial people with accounting degrees from corporate headquarters out into the field to get closer to the business. However, their recruiting policy has not changed.

Boeing and 3M also recruit from the undergraduate accounting programs in their metropolitan areas. At Boeing, particularly on the military side, accounting majors are giving way to computer science and statistics majors with stronger computer skills. In 3M there is some talk of hiring more MBAs, but there has been no substantial movement in that direction.

Another difference is that individuals start their professional careers in the two groups of firms at different ages. At Ford, Merck, and Citicorp, entry level is mid-to-late twenties. At AT&T, Boeing, and 3M, entry level is early twenties. To a certain extent, the firms positioned at or near the competitive-team model require people to have more work and/or educational experience before becoming a financial professional within the firm.

At those firms recruiting from the MBA or experienced CPA population, individuals have had the opportunity to develop their communication and interpersonal skills on the job or in a graduate education environment. The big six CPA firms and the graduate business schools round out the technically trained accounting and finance majors. Ford, Merck, and Citicorp encourage continued professional development of their financial professionals through in-house and external executive development programs.

Citicorp has a policy of trying to meet the demand for improvement in professional skills through sophisticated in-house training programs. Merck encourages professional development by building training and development into its executive compensation program. It has established a floor and a ceiling for professional development. Bonus points are awarded to financial professionals when they reach a minimum or floor level of training and development, and additional bonus points can be earned up to a maximum at the ceiling. At Merck, training and development are tied directly to the reward system.

It is interesting to observe that the Ford, Merck, and Citicorp cultures place the most emphasis on developing the capabilities of the individual financial professional. The AT&T, Boeing, and 3M cultures are still more oriented to systems, functions or tasks.

Any educational institution trying to meet the demands of the entire business community would have to develop a diversified strategy of undergraduate, graduate, and executive education programs. Given the scarcity of institutional resources, it is more likely that different schools will have to develop different target markets.

Since we have included only six large, highly visible firms in this research study, the natural question to ask is whether our findings can be applied to the broader financial community. In the next section, we provide evidence from the FERF study on "Development of Financial Executives," which leads us to believe that the two different recruiting strategies are reasonably representative of the broader FEI membership.

Developing Financial Executives

In a recent study commissioned by FERF, The Gallup Organization interviewed a sample of 1202 individuals by telephone during December, January, and February 1990. The study included:

☐ 402 senior financial executives—CFOs, senior vice presidents of finance, controllers, etc.

☐ 400 middle-level executives who have day-to-day contact with recently hired college and university graduates.

☐ 400 individuals, hired within the last three years, who were identified as having the potential to develop into senior-level financial executives.

For the purposes of our study, the demographic characteristics and the responses from the first two groups will help position the recruiting strategies of our six firms within the broader FEI membership. Here is a summary of the data from the 802 senior- and middle-level executives:

1. 59 percent have bachelor's degrees in accounting. An additional 24 percent have bachelor's degrees in economics, business administration, or finance.

2. 42.5 percent have advanced degrees. 32.5 percent have MBAs. 18.5 percent have their MBA major in finance. 10 percent have other master's degrees.

3. 57 percent have CPA certificates.

4. The importance of an advanced degree and/or the CPA certificate is expected to increase by the year 2000. 48.5 percent of the managerial staff in the financial organization are expected to have the advanced degree and 47.5 percent the CPA certificate. This is up from the current levels of 33.7 percent advanced degree and 37.9 percent CPA certificate.

5. 80 percent were recruited from outside the firm.

6. 64 percent of the senior- and middle-level financial executives believed that future senior level financial executives would come from internal development programs by the year 2000.

The Gallup survey data gave us the basis for a critique of the business curriculum and speculation about a new financial management major. We can see that any specific curricula changes will have to recognize:

1. The importance of the accounting major and degree within the corporate financial community.

2. The current and perceived increasing importance of an advanced degree (the MBA with an emphasis on finance) and the CPA certificate.

3. The fact that 80 percent of the financial executives are recruited from the outside.

4. The increased importance of developing senior financial executives in-house.

The responses by financial executives in the Gallup survey leave no doubt that knowledge of accounting is crucial to the success of a financial executive. However, we argue that knowledge of accounting takes on different dimensions within the conformance, command-and-control, and competitive-team orientations.

Critiquing the Current Accounting Curriculum

In this study, it became apparent to us that the current accounting curriculum does not recognize the trend toward competitive-team orientation in corporate financial work. Several of the firms in this study are moving toward a competitive-team orientation, or at least recognize the need to be more sensitive to a team culture. Yet we contend that the accounting curriculum remains firmly rooted in the conformance and command-and-control orientations.

The conformance orientation in accounting education is probably best exemplified by the phrase "prepared in conformity with generally accepted accounting principles." Financial accounting information is meant primarily for external use. Financial accounting courses focus on the rules and regulations that the organization must follow to fulfill its external accountability requirements.

The command-and-control orientation is probably best exemplified by the distinction made between financial and managerial accounting. Management accounting information is meant for internal use. Drawing from a typical management accounting text, management accounting information should "relate to that part of the company that the manager oversees." The structure of the curriculum supports and reinforces the concept of the conformance and command-and-control orientations. Also, when we maintain the distinctions between financial accounting, managerial accounting and tax accounting, for example, we further fortify the concept.

At present, we believe the accounting curriculum is lagging far behind the changes that are occurring within business. We start our critique with a discussion of the conformance orientation.

The Conformance Orientation

The predominant characteristic of undergraduate and graduate accounting programs is the conformance orientation. It concerns itself mainly with technical compliance with external rules and regulations.

The legitimacy and status of the financial professional is based on knowledge of the rules. The accountant is responsible for the technical and procedural administration of rules subject to internal and external compliance reviews. Over the years, the accounting curriculum has been dominated by course work in financial accounting, tax and auditing and not management control, finance and business strategy. Furthermore, schools of accountancy and accounting departments receive almost all of their external financial support from the large public accounting firms. The accounting curriculum conforms to the needs of the public accounting profession, the major employer of undergraduate accounting majors.

The strong conformance orientation is reflected in:

1. The number of course credits (18–21) devoted to financial accounting, tax and auditing.

2. The strong rule-driven pedagogy of these courses in which students are taught an encyclopedia of technical rules to follow in accounting for various types of financial transactions.

3. A faculty reward structure that assigns highest status to research in financial reporting and auditing.

The proliferation of statements of financial accounting standards has had the insidious effect of pushing the accounting curriculum in an ever more technical and ever less business-oriented direction. The curriculum has become devoted to teaching students the technical rules and conventions of conformance. More and more it concentrates on formal accounting rules, with correspondingly less focus on essential business and social issues.

Even within the public accounting profession, similar concerns have been raised about the state of accounting education. This view is confirmed by the Bedford Commission Report (American Accounting Association, 1986; Bedford and Shenkir, 1987), the recent position paper by the big eight (now six) public accounting firms(Arthur, Anderson and Co., et al., 1989), and the charge to the Accounting Education Change Commission (Mueller and Simmons, 1989).

If the experiences of AT&T and Citicorp provide any indication of what it takes to break a conformance mentality, we may have to wait for a major upheaval before accounting programs in business schools will make any effective movement away from the conformance orientation. It may take deregulation in the public accounting industry or a shrinking of auditing revenues and an increase in importance of value-added client service activities at the big six accounting firms.

The Command-and-Control Orientation

The conventional management accounting side of the curriculum has tended to reflect and reinforce the highly functional character of the command-and-control orientation. It emphasizes a set of formal techniques for budgeting and cost analysis that is poorly integrated with substantive operational and strategic management issues. Traditionally, management accounting course work has not been integrated with course work in industrial economics, business strategy, finance, or operations management. As a result, management accounting students are taught to believe that accountants have a proprietary right to budgeting and cost control. Therefore, they have no need to develop a broad appreciation of competitive strategy, market dynamics, or the impact of new manufacturing technologies on management practices. Those concerns are someone else's functional responsibility.

Possibly the most telling indication of the strong command-and-control orientation of management accounting is the pervasive use of the principal-agent concept for modeling and controlling human behavior. This principal-agent concept conceives of the firm as a system of formal, hierarchically-structured contracts among self-interested parties. The model presupposes a climate of distance, distrust, and information asymmetry. Under this concept of the firm, a big task of the management accountant is to design and administer an independent information system designed to monitor and control agent opportunism.

While there are many legitimate applications of the agency theory in business, it is most definitely a partial view of organizational dynamics. Accordingly, we question its utility as the major guide for educating students who will join firms moving toward the competitive-team orientation. If the principal-agent model stands predominant among research-oriented management accounting faculty, it stands to reason that it would tend to predominate faculty thinking, teaching, and perceptions of business managers.

The new emphasis on cost management has created an impetus for change in the orientation and content of the management accounting curriculum. Triggered in part by the work of Robert Kaplan and his colleagues at Harvard, a new awareness appears to be developing among educators that the management accounting curriculum must be restructured. It must give students a broader understanding of the relationship among competitive strategy, manufacturing technologies, business processes, and measurement systems.

Signs of change are encouraging, but we would strike at least one note of caution. While accountants are talking about what new methods of activity costing can be used and how to integrate these new methods into the curriculum, a more profound change is not really being addressed. This study demonstrates that the role of the management accountant is changing as the boundaries break down among engineering, manufacturing, and financial control. As management moves toward a more team-oriented model of workplace organization, management accountants must recognize that cost management and stewardship responsibility over resources are not just accounting concerns. As concepts of ownership and responsibility are pushed down through the organization, the role of the management accountant is bound to change dramatically.

The Ford story and, to a lesser extent, the AT&T story clearly demonstrate that firms faced with severe economic crisis or intense global competition are making massive reductions in financial staff. These reductions are taking place where accounting controls and operating relationships can be streamlined and computerized without impeding the decision-making process. It just might take a massive lack of market acceptance of command-and-control oriented accounting majors to bring about changes in the curriculum.

The Competitive-Team Orientation

Neither the conformance orientation nor the command-and-control orientation seems likely to produce a team-oriented individual with the educational foundation needed to develop into a financial professional—a professional who is expected to move out from the back office or out from the front office onto the playing field. To become a value-adding member of the business team, an accounting-educated, financial professional must learn to think positively in shaping business decisions. Such a professional must be taught how to integrate technical accounting knowledge, coupled with an understanding of finance and economics, into a corporate business context.

The present accounting curriculum does not satisfactorily develop the proper psychological inclination, communication skills, nor a healthy attitude toward problem-solving and life-long learning. Nor does it cultivate the breadth and depth of knowledge that is expected from a team-oriented corporate financial professional. An accounting curriculum designed to develop a team-oriented financial professional would be quite different, perhaps radically different, from the present curriculum. The changes would have to be similar to the changes financial organizations are undergoing as they shift to the competitive-team orientation.

Speculating About a Different Curriculum

We believe that several short-term modifications could be made to the accounting curriculum that would go a long way toward developing the financial professional educated to be a member of a competitive team:

1. Just as firms are facing up to the dysfunctional character of organizational chimneys, educators must face up to the problems caused by disciplinary chimneys. We believe it is worthwhile to consider the development of an accounting-based financial management major with more emphasis placed on business problem-solving and less emphasis placed on conformity to rules and oversight.

   The course curriculum must become highly streamlined and integrated, to leave ample room for liberal arts and social science electives. For instance, we believe that the corporate demand for undergraduates with sound technical accounting skills can be met with fewer accounting course credits than are now required. A more conceptual and streamlined treatment of technical material would emphasize simplification and integration similar to what Ford is doing as a result of the Mazda studies.

2. Substantive topics would be taught from a business perspective instead of a disciplinary perspective. The concept of getting close to the business, applied within the curriculum, would mean that students would be taught how to integrate the formal logic and techniques of accounting, economics, and finance with a basic understanding of the products, markets, and competitive strategies of the business.

3. Since getting close to the business requires more exposure to actual business practices and problems, firms adopting the competitive-team orientation would have to recognize their responsibility for supporting the students and faculty involved with this new major. If financial executives want to influence the direction that undergraduate and graduate education takes in the future, they must make a moral and financial commitment of support, similar to the support provided by the big six public accounting firms over the last three decades.

On the academic side of any new corporate commitment, individual faculty members must become more responsive to integrating form and substance in the classroom. We believe that current doctoral programs in accounting and finance must be restructured to develop faculty with the ability to integrate specialized technical expertise within a business context. Currently, PhD students and young faculty members are often counseled to avoid field research because it is too time-consuming or because field research is not an acceptable scientific endeavor. As a result of this bias, young faculty are discouraged from "getting close to the business world," from gaining a firsthand appreciation of a business world that can be brought into the classroom. We believe that a broadening of the accepted paradigm of accounting research is an essential change required to attract and reward the type of faculty who are qualified to educate the team-oriented financial professional.

Section B

Contents

Introduction

Individual Firm Stories

The six individual firm stories presented in Section B are sequenced in the following manner: Ford, Merck, Citicorp, 3M, AT&T, and Boeing[1]. The Ford, Merck, and Citicorp stories exemplify how three financial organizations have moved toward the competitive-team model of financial work. The 3M, AT&T, and Boeing stories exemplify more traditional types of financial organizations, with more emphasis on the command-and-control and conformance orientation to financial work. The interviews with AT&T executives indicate that the financial organization is moving toward the competitive-team orientation. However, AT&T is not as far along as Ford, Merck, and Citicorp, and the AT&T story has been positioned between the 3M and Boeing stories to emphasize their most recent history between command-and-control and conformance.

Ford

The Ford story documents a movement away from a strong command-and-control orientation to a competitive-team orientation induced in part by the need to become more cost competitive with the Japanese automakers. The interviews at Ford provided the initial basis for identifying the key elements of the command-and-control and competitive-team orientations. The movement away from an independent, functionally-oriented finance staff toward a financial organization that is integrated into the business operations was particularly evident at Ford. The interviews at Ford were particularly important in establishing the fact that a major American corporation can make a dramatic turnaround when faced with a severe economic crisis. Between 1979 and 1987, the financial organization experienced a 40 percent reduction in salaried head count—a greater reduction than the overall corporation. A substantial part of the successful reduction in salaried head count can be attributed to the lessons learned by Ford executives in detailed studies conducted at Mazda in the early 1980s.

[1]The firm stories are largely based on interviews of company executives. The titles of the executives cited were their titles at the time of the interviews.

Merck

The Merck story documents the movement away from a muted command-and-control orientation to a competitive-team orientation. In Merck's case, the financial organization has embraced the R&D spirit of the scientists and researchers developing new ethical drugs. The Merck story emphasizes the commitment on behalf of the CFO to develop an organization of financial professionals who are expected to make a measurable, individual, value-added contribution to Merck's bottom line. Merck's financial organization prides itself on having developed a highly sophisticated R&D planning model to help the scientists and researchers target their new product development efforts.

Citicorp

The Citicorp story documents the movement away from a conformance orientation toward a competitive-team orientation. Like Merck, Citicorp encourages individual, value-added involvement with the business units. The interviews at Citicorp helped us develop the imagery of "team" as athletic team versus team as family. If you don't perform on the field, you will be replaced. In particular, the Citicorp interviews provided concrete evidence of the type of contribution a financial control professional makes to the team in the financial services industry. Terms like "financial engineering" and "accounting risk" refer to the type of value-added contributions that financial professionals make to the team at Citicorp.

3M

The 3M story documents the challenges faced by a financial organization positioned between a command-and-control orientation and a competitive-team orientation. The senior financial management group at 3M faces two significant challenges: 1) the challenge of being involved with the business units while maintaining an independent corporate perspective; and 2) the challenge of supporting the business unit customers while continuing to reduce the costs of providing financial services through the use of the latest computer technology. Of all the firms included in the study, 3M's financial function appears to be the most systems-oriented. Its commodity P&L system is the backbone of 3M's financial control system.

AT&T

As mentioned briefly above, the AT&T story documents a financial organization attempting to adjust, along with everyone else in AT&T, to the transition from being a regulated domestic monopoly to becoming a deregulated global competitor. AT&T's financial function, which was once described as a complex bookkeeping operation devoted to the technical administration of externally imposed rules and regulations, is now trying to become a professional financial organization emphasizing sophisticated financial analysis and support to the business units. The AT&T interviews were the most helpful in fleshing out the elements of the conformance orientation. Although the AT&T executives point out that the previous culture was also command-and-control, the most difficult task facing AT&T is moving away from a conformance mindset.

Boeing

The Boeing story documents the active presence of all three financial function orientations within the same firm. The corporate financial group is firmly positioned between command-and-control and conformance. The financial organization on the commercial side is primarily command-and-control with some movement toward competitive-team. While the financial organization on the military side is moving from a conformance orientation toward the competitive-team orientation. The Boeing story is a story of three very different cultures coexisting within the same organization. Boeing was asked to participate in the study because of its mix of commercial and government business. As just mentioned, we found significant differences between the two sides of the business, but not for the reasons one might expect.

We would like to reemphasize that the financial executives within each firm have had the opportunity to review their individual stories within the context of the conceptual model developed in Chapter 4 and, possibly more important, within the context of the stories told about each of the other firms. Each firm has, in effect, "signed off" on how its financial organization would be presented to their peers in other corporations and to educators and researchers interested in patterns of variation and change in corporate America.

1
Ford

The story of the financial function at Ford over the past ten years is one of dramatic change, both quantitative and qualitative in character. Quantitatively, the finance organization was some 40 percent smaller in 1987 than it was in 1979. This reduction occurred as part of an overall downsizing of productive and administrative staffing at Ford. A particularly noteworthy statistic in this regard is that salaried administrative head count either remained constant or decreased for thirty-five out of the thirty-six quarters from 1979-1987. The finance organization played a significant part in this downsizing effort. Over that period, the financial organization experienced a 40 percent reduction in salaried head count—a greater reduction than the overall corporation.

The early stages of the staff reductions in finance were accomplished through across-the-board cuts and organizational consolidations. Current reductions are being accomplished through a qualitative shift in the orientation of the financial organization. Under its historical command-and-control orientation, the financial organization structure was designed primarily to monitor and oversee the decisions and work practices of the line operations. As Ford reoriented its entire culture to foster more team-oriented decision-making and work practices, the historical over-the-shoulder monitoring and overstaffing that such an orientation had created, have become unnecessary. The fundamental reorientation of the finance organization into a group of team players has contributed to significant reductions in head count.

Given its declining performance in the marketplace and stimulated by what Ford learned in studies conducted at Mazda, top management came to realize that its entire command-and-control culture and the inefficiencies that this culture had bred, was not competitive. In the early to mid '80s, top management initiated a series of efforts to reorient the culture from a historical command-and-control orientation to a competitive-team orientation. This change in culture is producing dramatic effects in effects in how Ford approaches its engineering, production, and administrative work practices. Given the centralized orientation of the financial function under the command-and-control orientation, it is not surprising that the financial work practices within Ford have undergone the most profound change. This case documents the nature of these changes and describes how the change in orientation directly influenced the organization of financial work within the firm.

The Shift from Command-and-Control to Competitive-Team

The first formal business plan produced by Ford's corporate finance staff outlined the financial organization's objectives and productivity plans. The plan documented the shift from corporate confrontation and perceived "second guessing" as a mode of operation to being supportive and playing an active role in the operating unit decision-making process. The business plan documents the effect of this shift in orientation on the pattern of work and allocation of resources within the function:

> In keeping with changes throughout the company, finance staff began a move in the early 1980s to reduce its review function, and to increase its direct involvement in development work with the operations. Much of the analytical work performed by finance staff dealing with business restructuring and competitive analysis is done for the benefit of the operations and corporate management . . . Finance staff has reallocated its resources away from the more traditional review functions. We continue to perform a review function, but the resource allocation in the area has been reduced. (Finance Business Plan, p. 1)

> In the past, finance staff's role in fulfilling its responsibilities to central corporate management often was perceived as a "Staff Review" function. The company's operating philosophy has been changing over time to reflect an increased emphasis on employee involvement at all levels, and delegation of more responsibility and authority to the operations. As the company has been changing, so too has finance staff. Finance staff generally is seen by its customers as a contributing member of the company's team.

> To improve upon the changes in this role, [it has been suggested] that finance staff expand its efforts to understand the operations, including more developmental assignments in the manufacturing divisions. It was believed that these efforts would be productive and could reduce perceived "second guessing" of operating plans. (Finance Business Plan, p. 3)

These statements provide direct evidence of an explicit shift in organizational mission and a recognition that finance staff must interrelate with line management in carrying out that mission. These statements suggest a prior pattern of work relations and practices emphasizing oversight and review, which reinforces the view that finance staff was the enforcer of corporate management controls. The business plan indicates that this pattern of post-hoc monitoring and review, characteristic of a command-and-control orientation, is being de-emphasized as the financial organization moves to a competitive-team orientation.

Under the competitive-team orientation, the focus has shifted emphasis from internal monitoring to external market analysis. The greatest threat to corporate success is no longer perceived to be internal line management and employees, but the external competition, especially the Japanese. Accordingly, the finance organization is focusing its efforts and reallocating its resources from "downstream" oversight to "upstream" involvement in the formulation and management of competitive strategy. The business plan documents numerous ongoing efforts to upgrade competitive analysis and acquisition analysis. Finance staff is also trying to incorporate difficult-to-quantify "qualitative" factors into its financial analysis, a significant change from the past.

The excerpts from the Finance Business Plan contain the essential elements of the shift in orientation from a command-and-control to a competitive-team orientation. Fundamentally, the shift is from the role of overseer of corporate policies and procedures, and conservator of corporate resources to that of business advisor and partner. And, in aspiring to be valued as a "team player" rather than a "goal tender" (Finance Business Plan, p. 3), finance staff's legitimacy has shifted from its location in the organizational hierarchy to legitimacy based on expertise. Finance staff no longer has the power to veto proposals from operations.

The Competitive Imperative for Change

The 40 percent staff reductions mentioned above were initiated by Ford to become more cost competitive with Japanese automakers. Ford management was aware that its small car costs were significantly higher than Japanese-manufactured vehicles sold in the United States, and that survival of the company depended on rectifying this situation. From 1977–1979, Ford experienced substantial losses in market share.

Conditions turned from bad to worse during the 1980–1982 period, when Ford experienced three consecutive years of operating losses. During this period, it was not clear whether Ford had the time or resources to turn things around.

Top management was faced with the imperative of radically changing its business practices in order to produce a car that could meet the standards of the Japanese imports. The alternative was not doing business at all. Everyone within Ford shared a common interest in averting the crisis. In reflecting back on the stimuli to change, Ken Coates, Controller of Diversified Products Operations, put it this way:

> It was a combination of two things. It was an environment where because of some of our past sins plus the second oil crisis plus the recession in the economy, we were in deep trouble financially. At the same time, we discovered that we had a whole host of new competitors who had different cost structures, different work ethics, different methodologies, and who were coming in and eating our lunch. So it was the combination of those two pressures. I'm not certain that one of those alone would have been enough. The combination of those two literally created a crisis where we said, we don't know if we're going to make it. From a competitive stand-point, we were saying, we can't do business the way we've been doing business; it won't work anymore because the guy out there is doing it faster, cheaper, and better than we are. And that's what drove the [change in] orientation.

Ken Coates reflected on the implications for the finance organization:

> But we got to the crux of the early 1980s and we were on death's door. And we quickly got to the point where we said, we can't afford to have this huge finance organization doing things that really should be done by the operating organizations. Because there was some duplication of effort there. And obviously, [there] was this huge papermill through the financial control process—from operating people to finance people back to operating people . . .

> We just looked at ourselves and said, we've got this huge administrative structure associated here and we're fat. And we compared ourselves with the Japanese manufacturers, who didn't have anything even remotely resembling the kind of financial control system we have. We said, we can't afford to do that anymore. We now have to compete with those guys. And they are managing to turn out products that have their costs controlled. They're doing it in a very different way from what we're doing. And that's where the whole cultural thing comes in . . .

With a full view of history, with 20/20 hindsight, change might appear to have occurred in a more orderly fashion than actually was the case. At the time, the initial decision to reduce staff was made without a specific understanding of how to work smarter and more efficiently. The economic crisis required top management to administer radical surgery by instituting across-the-board staff reductions. Taking the lead in this regard, finance staff set a target of cutting its own head count by 25 percent within five years.

Survival demanded drastic action. The question was, however, in what specific ways were Japanese automakers more cost competitive? To a certain extent, there was a natural tendency for different functions within Ford to point the finger at each other as the cause of inefficiency.

The Mazda Studies: A Different and Better Way

A major turning point for Ford occurred in the early 1980s when Mazda (who was a major Ford supplier and in whom Ford had a 25 percent ownership share) agreed to permit Ford staff to conduct extensive and detailed analyses of Mazda's operations. An initial study produced by Ford's financial organization documented the fact that there was a dramatic difference in cost structures between the two firms, permitting Japanese automakers to land a car in the U.S. for significantly less than Ford could produce a similar car domestically. Dick Cook, General Assistant Controller, described everyone's initial refusal to believe the difference in the cost structures between the two firms. The $2,600 figure mentioned below refers to the difference in production cost between the two firms, a difference that was becoming progressively greater in favor of the Japanese automaker:

> It wasn't long before the figure was $2,600. People started to believe. [Their reaction was,] tell me what the elements are: engine, transmission, assembly, every cockeyed element of this thing, and finance. Five of us went over [to Mazda] in 1981. We couldn't believe what we heard. We knew at that time that we had twice as many people as we ought to have. We said we ought to reduce [head count] by a third. People [at Ford] laughed, but the momentum kept building.

The analyses that followed the initial visit to Mazda were helpful in two ways. The analyses permitted detailed comparisons of distinct functions within Ford and within Mazda. With these comparisons, Ford was able to 1) identify those functions most in need of improvement, thereby eliminating the finger-pointing among the various functions, and 2) learn from Mazda the specific methods and techniques needed to effect those improvements. The full set of function-specific studies led to recommendations for dramatic across-the-board changes at all levels within Ford: manufacturing, engineering, production control, finance and accounting, and industrial relations.

Substantial differences were found in the size and organization of the accounting function between Ford and Mazda [Mazda Comparison Study, Phase IIB, 1986, hereafter referred to as the Mazda Comparison Study]. The Ford study team concluded that there were about seven times as many people performing comparable accounting functions at North American Automotive Operations (NAAO) than at Mazda. While the study team did not attempt to adjust this difference for the relative size of the two organizations, it did note that the difference provided no evidence of economies of scale that might be expected given Ford's greater size. In fact, the study indicated exactly the opposite. Mazda produced almost three times as many cars per accounting employee as Ford.

The Mazda Comparison Study noted five broad areas of difference between accounting activities at Ford and Mazda:

1) Mazda's internal and external reporting was less complex than Ford's. While Ford's accounting supported a more dispersed number of legal entities and internal profit centers, it also entailed more formal controls, procedures, and reporting requirements.

2) Mazda's general and cost accounting activities were centralized, whereas Ford's were decentralized at the division and plant levels.

3) Mazda's operating and accounting systems were integrated with common data bases, whereas Ford's were not.

4) Many accounting activities performed by the financial organization within Ford were performed by operating units at Mazda. Ford found that the dispersion of these activities at Mazda "is a long-standing arrangement consistent with the idea of assigning responsibility to activities that have authority and operational control."

5) Mazda's accountants were less specialized and thus prepared to handle a greater variety of activities, including analytical work, whereas at Ford the distinction between accounting and analysis had been rather distinct, with little cross-over between the separate career tracks.

The Mazda Comparison Study led in turn to recommendations for top management to consider 1) the elimination of internal profit centers, 2) simplifying, consolidating, and commonizing the accounting systems (this recommendation to be accompanied by substantial projected head count reductions), 3) reassigning accounting functions to non-finance activities to reduce the compartmentalization and redundancy of accounting activities, and 4) expanding the development and training of accounting personnel.

The Influence of Operating Philosophy on the Organization of Financial Work

As a result of studying Mazda, Ford management came to realize that its differences with Mazda were not simply at the level of practices and procedures. Differences in operating practices and procedures were the product and embodiment of a radically different operating philosophy. Thus, Ford sought to understand "how Mazda's philosophies influence operating procedures and salaried employees within the organization." With respect to the accounting function, the Mazda Study Team concluded that "the comparison of functions performed by accountants at Ford and Mazda showed major differences in organization, philosophy, and assignment of responsibilities." The Mazda Comparison Study described an entirely different team-oriented approach to financial work at Mazda, which in turn produced the radically simpler pattern of accounting systems and staffing.

The Mazda Study Team concluded that Mazda's efficiency gains resulted from dispersing many so-called accounting activities to non-finance functions. Mazda's management philosophy assumed an underlying degree of trust and teamwork among organizational activities within the organization. Quoting from the study:

> It is evident from the way Mazda is organized and assigns accounting-related functions to non-finance activities, that there is a high degree of trust and teamwork between organizations. This environment helps eliminate duplication of effort. Mazda activities handle a broad range of responsibilities related to their operation, and it is not necessary for detailed information to be passed to accounting for processing, data entry, and reporting. This philosophy differs from Ford's where accounting is performed and controls are monitored predominantly within the finance organization.

The study team concluded that an operating philosophy character-ized by consensus (shared values), trust, and a high level of employee commitment exerted a substantial influence on the staffing, organization, and distribution of financial work throughout Mazda. The study team also concluded that this operating philosophy results in streamlined and more effective control systems. In essence, this finding is consistent with Ouchi's argument about the efficiency of a clan culture (Ouchi, 1987).

The study team concluded that Mazda's operating philosophy does not require a control system populated by additional personnel to administer checks and balances, because responsibility for productivity and cost control is lodged in each and every organizational subunit and employee, rather than with the financial organization as in Ford. Control is placed where it can be most effectively and efficiently performed—at the level and with the individuals who perform the activity. Thus, Ford concluded that to realize the potential benefits of its analyses of Mazda's operating practices it must revise its operating philosophy as well. As Dave Barry, head of a special finance unit on process improvement at the time of the interviews, put it:

> In Japan, the Japanese engineer is responsible for the complete job . . . He con-trols the cost. He controls the variable costs of the vehicle. He does the whole job. And the finance people are the ones who pay the bills and give him reports periodically on what all those costs added up to, but they are not really control-ling the costs. So over time, we have been shifting, sometimes rapidly, sometimes slowly, much more toward a mindset that the operating people are the only ones who can really control the costs, and that they should be controlling the costs; that's part of their job. Why separate costs from all the other things they do, because all the other things they do determine what the costs are? So [we] should get the cost responsibility over there where it belongs. Cut down the size of the finance organi-zation. Then use the finance organization for the things only it can do.

It is hard to overestimate the impact that the Mazda studies have had on Ford. The handwriting was on the wall. The Mazda studies made the handwriting understandable and showed Ford management a different and a better way. The Mazda studies helped Ford to understand how its own practices had become institutionalized, but were not necessary to the technical task requirements. The Mazda studies demonstrated the need for a change of mindset, or orientation, to financial work. In these studies, we find the hard evidence to support Ford management's com-mitment to the shift from a command-and-control orientation to a com-petitive-team orientation.

The Mazda studies concretely documented the relationship between finance-function orientation and the costs of financial work. In fact, Ford used these studies as a basis for reconfiguring productive and administrative work practices at the plant level. Ford put these new practices into operation on a pilot basis in its stamping and assembly plant in Hermisillo, Mexico. Based on intensive studies conducted at the Hermisillo plant, new productivity targets for hourly and salaried head count were established for all plant-level operations.

At the corporate level, the Mazda studies provided a knowledge base upon which to plan further reductions beyond the initial cuts made in administrative (including financial) staffing. By the time of the completion of the Mazda studies, Ford had accomplished its initial across-the-board cuts. But these cuts were done by edict, and did not effect any real organizational change other than a leaner, but not necessarily stronger, company. Ford recognized that its cost structure, even after these cuts, was still not cost competitive. Ford wished to exploit what it had learned from Mazda. Knowledge to simplify accounting and control procedures gained from the Mazda studies could be used to make further reductions in financial staffing. As the Mazda Comparison Study noted:

> Ford is working to reduce costs on many fronts, but salaried personnel reductions have a unique priority because salaried staffing levels are indicative of the efficiency and effectiveness of a company's entire operating system. . . .
>
> The salaried personnel reductions NAAO has made since 1979 mostly represent more efficient operation of ongoing systems and procedures. Accomplishment of the reductions still needed will require that systems and procedures be simplified and changed so that fewer people are required to maintain operational effectiveness.

Based on the information from the Mazda studies, Ford finance has undertaken a major thrust in financial systems simplification, consolidation, and commonization, with the objective of reducing accounting staff by 25 percent over the time period 1986–1990. For instance, the Mazda Comparison Study estimated that Ford could cut its NAAO accounts payable staffing by about 80 percent through systems simplification, consolidation and commonization. This effort has been undertaken, and Ford is well on its way toward realizing this goal. The extent of Ford's commitment to system simplification is indicated by the special unit on process improvement established within the corporate finance function.

As indicated in preceding paragraphs, Ford's finance staff realized that the streamlined financial systems at Mazda were the product of a much broader team-oriented operating philosophy, characterized by greater trust of employees and less specialization of administrative work. This philosophy minimizes the amount of checks and balances, and hierarchical oversight required to insure proper execution of function. To fully appreciate the significance of this shift in orientation and its potential impact on extant patterns of financial work at Ford, one must place it in the context of the history of Ford's command-and-control management style and pattern of intra-management and labor-management relations. A description of this history is provided in the next section.

Command-and-Control: The Historical Orientation of Financial Management at Ford

In many senses, Ford has epitomized the predominant pattern of mass production and organization found in American firms, the so-called machine bureaucracy (Mintzberg, 1979; Miller and Friesen, 1984). The machine bureaucracy is characterized by extreme division of labor and a command-and-control orientation to the management of the firm. Forged during the Henry Ford era of mass production in the early part of this century, this command-and-control philosophy has come under increasingly heavy criticism as analysts have sought to understand how weaknesses of American managerial practices are contributing to the declining competitiveness of American industry. The Japanese car industry has proven there is a better way to organize for mass production. In fact, it could be argued that the success of the Japanese automakers represented the first definitive demonstration that bureaucratic control and extreme task specialization are not inextricable aspects of competitive mass production methods. The authors of the important new book *Made in America* argue this point:

> The great success of the American economy in the twentieth century was a system of mass production of standard products for a large domestic market. The system turned out a large volume of goods at low cost. It also provided jobs that paid well and were fairly stable, except for recurring economy-wide recessions. The success of mass production was most dramatic in the American automobile industry, which was once the envy of the world. (Dertouzos, 1989, p. 47)

The success of the Japanese car industry is based on a system different in almost every feature from Detroit's mass-production system. The Japanese have succeeded by providing different products for each segment of the market. To do so efficiently and profitably, they have developed technologies, product-development methods, and patterns of workplace organization that allow them to reduce the volume of production and increase the speed with which new products are brought to market.(Dertouzos, 1989, p. 48)

Because of its perceived success over the past fifty years, the command-and-control operating philosophy and the related patterns of productive work and financial control have become embedded into the very fabric of management and labor relations in American industry. The institutionalized nature of these attitudes and work practices both shape and constrain efforts to affect a new operating philosophy.

Like many other American firms, Ford could be characterized as an organization lulled into stagnancy and a false sense of competitive strength by a post-war economic performance, related more to the material strength and physical might of the U.S. political economy, than to its own engineering and managerial prowess. As the 1970s wore on, the weaknesses of Ford's command-and-control operating philosophy became progressively more obvious. A feature of this operating philosophy, and thus a central—but by no means sole—part of the problem, lies in the role of the finance function in the management of the firm.

Interestingly, in his best-selling book *The Reckoning* David Halberstam portrays Ford as a firm that embodied many of the dysfunctionalities of "managing-by-the-numbers." He portrays Ford's finance staff as propagating a system of financial control and oversight that had gradually suffocated the firm's capacity to innovate. The rise and fall of the financial organization is a central feature of Halberstam's story.

The roots of finance staff's power go back to the Ford turnaround after the World War II years and the role played by the finance whiz kids during that era. The history of financial work begins with Henry Ford, who, as Halberstam notes, hated accountants so much that he left his grandson, Henry Ford II, with a company in absolute financial despair. In an effort to impose desperately needed financial discipline into the failing company, Henry Ford II recruited one of GM's top financial executives, Ernie Breech, and the now-famous whiz kids. Their mixture of finance and systems analysis proved to have a very interesting and powerful chemistry.

In bringing Ernie Breech to his firm, Henry Ford brought Alfred Sloan's management philosophy, system of financial management, and strong advisory staffs. In attempting to explain Ford's heavy investment of resources in the control of the car development process, Ken Coates (Controller of Diversified Products Operations) referred to Sloan's philosophy of control and its inherent relation to the character of the industry:

> It's a combination of things. Part of it is historical and, to some extent, industry practice. The best way to start explaining it, I think, is to go back to Sloan's concept of how he wanted to manage GM. It was basically, you control the money and you control the people . . . In the automotive business, the investment required to change products, even to re-skin them, is very significant . . . In an environment like that, the potential for blowing it and spending too much, or getting creamed by suppliers is very significant. So you want to devote a lot of resources to trying to control that . . . Sloan's philosophy, as best I remember it, was fundamentally: O.K., you tell the people out there how much they have to spend for a product program. It's kind of like, you cut the suit to fit the cloth. So he would control what the organization did by how much spending they were permitted to do and how many people they got.

Very high strategic risk, coupled with the constraints on capital, demand strong control over the use of resources. These conditions predispose top management to develop a strong complement of financial advisory staff members. In his book *GM Passes Ford,* Kuhn argues that the superiority of Sloan's management philosophy over that of Henry Ford's was the reason why GM surpassed Ford as the dominant automaker in the 1930s. Ford did not have a cadre of sophisticated management professionals schooled in the best engineering and financial management practices:

> The widely differing design philosophies found within the two firms can be traced ultimately to the degree of systematic technical training and scientific education attained by their key participants. At GM, the principals represented an emerging breed of engineering-oriented executives who were rationalizing the American system of corporate capitalism. (1986, p. 5)

Certainly, the whiz kids fit this paradigm and complemented the skills that Breech brought to Ford. With their success in turning Ford around in those post World War II years, the whiz kids solidified a new paradigm of management at Ford. Having demonstrated the value of their capacity to bring financial discipline to a very complex organization, and their success in recruiting the best and the brightest who gradually filled Ford's top management ranks, finance staff gradually assumed the dominant position of power within Ford. In the words of Stan Seneker, the current CFO:

> I think the history of the finance function at Ford is that we've developed a repu-
> tation of having a very strong influence on the company over the years. I think
> we're all proud of this heritage, a pretty good success story for finance. When
> Henry Ford II brought in GM people and the whiz kids, there was a great empha-
> sis on financial control because it was the weakest part at that time. The financial
> influence was self-perpetuated because . . . finance was able to focus on getting
> the very best people. They were able to build a reputation right into the finance
> organization for being an influence on the company . . . Not just keeping the
> accounting records, but having an influence on business decisions, being
> involved in business decisions. That tended to attract good business school grad-
> uates. And so it was self-perpetuating . . . Once you get some very good people
> here—and they had a lot of very good people over the years—they then tend to
> influence the company.

Much of the credit for the influence of the finance staff goes to Edward Lundy, one of the original whiz kids and long-standing CFO of the firm. Mr. Lundy placed great importance on staff development and loyalty. The result was a highly coherent and very influential group. As one indicator of the importance Mr. Lundy placed on development, finance has its own personnel function. Ken Coates, who headed this function at one point in his career, also spoke of the influence of finance.

> The finance organization has done—and I think virtually anyone in the company
> will agree with this—by far the best job of recruiting, training, etc., people. This
> company has finance people scattered all over it in key jobs because the finance
> function historically has done the best recruiting and development job.

But possibly, finance did too good of a job. Possibly, finance became too powerful, and financial systems and numbers came to dominate product and manufacturing perspectives. Halberstam argues that the tradition of financial control as it evolved under the tutelage of Robert Mac-Namara and Edward Lundy went awry; possibly it focused too much on protecting the Ford family's assets. Second, it condoned arm-length control practices in which knowledge of the numbers was divorced from knowledge of product and firsthand experience with product design and manufacturing. Premised as they were upon distrust, these control systems functioned by intent as a counterbalance to the lack of rigor and discipline finance-oriented people observed in those who designed and managed the product, as well as in the waste and abuse in the manufacturing plants. The pattern of control and finance staffing that developed over time was a product of this distrust.

The Costs of Conflict and Distrust

To a certain extent, the check-and-balance dynamic of stewardship carries with it a certain inherent tension between the finance and line functions and, thus, the potential for conflict. As the current CFO put it:

> Both Mr. Peterson and Mr. Polling [current CEO and COO] view finance as the conscience of the company, if you want to put it that way. Operating people understand that if finance agrees, you move forward; if finance does not, you really take a second look.

> The problem you have, as with any finance organization, is that finance is viewed as the keeper of the keys, the money, the one who holds the budgets, the monetary strength of the company. And therefore, when something financially doesn't measure up and it gets turned down . . . it is viewed as, well, this was a great idea, and it would have made a great contribution to our product, but the finance guys turned it off. They have complex financial measures and turnover ratios, measures and turns and all of the finance jargon. Clearly you need financial controls; [it] would be an anarchy here if you didn't have financial controls . . . Are they cooperative controls that lead people to do the very best they can or are they inhibitors, burdens?

The language that interviewees used to describe the historical role of the finance function and its relationship with line management indicates that the practice of stewardship at Ford had evolved or, put more strongly, had hardened into a dynamic of distrust and enforcement. As one interviewee put it:

> Ten years ago, I think we had what I would call a cops-and-robbers mentality. The finance people were the cops. The engineers and the manufacturing people were the robbers. There was the mindset that the cops had to check everything that the other people did because, basically, the robbers were out there intentionally doing bad things. They wanted to spend too much money. They wanted to spend it in the wrong places. They didn't want to do it on the right things; they just had the wrong interests of the company at heart. But we, the cops, we're out there and we know the truth . . . We're going to protect the company.

In talking about the difference between the current team orientation and the older confrontational style of management, another interviewee put it this way:

> What is changing is that now you are exercising that power within team concept, rather than exercising it in a confrontational strategy . . . The original model that somebody set up years and years ago was sales people sold, finance people made sure it was a good price. And so you had a battle between the two people. The theory was you [got a] good compromise. In other words, I did get a reasonable price for the product I was going to sell.

> This confrontation was an integral part of the way we ran our business. We balanced operational requirements with financial requirements by confrontation at every level . . . when I joined the company, it was 100 percent expected.

In comments of interviewees at Ford, the use of such terms as, "cops and robbers," "policeman," "arm of the Board," "conscience of the company," "keeper of the keys," and even "dictator" conveyed the financial function's historical role within the command-and-control style of management at Ford. Each of these terms is quite suggestive of the climate of confrontation and distrust, in addition to the finance role as the conservator of the company's resources. In its role as conservator, the finance function's power and prestige came to be based much more on its position than its expertise. Thus, while Ford's financial management took pride in hiring the best and the brightest, its source of power and status was heavily based on its advisory function to top corporate management, and its power of budgetary veto over program proposals. One interviewee, while drawing a contrast between the former command-and-control role of finance and its current role under a team-oriented concept of management, explained:

> You go back to the Sloan model: I'm going to control this place through money and people. Well, your agents for controlling the money are finance people and for controlling the people are the personnel people. So you have those two organizations report to the CEO, not the COO . . . That's a very critical point. So, you have finance and personnel people think, hey we are off here to the side. We really are an arm of the CEO and the Board . . . but one of the difficulties with this company and, I think the auto industry in general, was those roles were very clearly defined, sharply defined. But it is clear to us that that created a lot of tension; there wasn't teamwork. People got to the point where they said, that is not my role, It's not my role to control costs, it's what those finance people are for. They are there to control costs. And we tended to foster that. It's a lot more inter-

esting if you control all of the money . . . We tended to favor the people who were eager in pursuing that role. And over time, the organizations grew apart in mindset of how they worked together.

The lesson from Ford's history may be that in an adversarial climate, the stewardship role as an integral part of a system of checks and balances, can harden into a dynamic of confrontation and enforcement. The result, simply put, is bad business.

Where adversarial relations exist, it is hard to perform the review function from a distance. Confrontation entails drawing lines and defending one's turf. It presumes and begets a climate of distrust and builds boundaries and barriers to communication. It divides and fragments. For Ford's finance staff, the dysfunctionality of management by confrontation was brought into unfavorable relief in comparison to Mazda. It manifested itself in hard dollars and cents on the bottom line and, more immediate, in the costs of financial control. It manifested itself in the poor quality of communication within Ford, and the poor quality and high cost of automobiles being produced.

There is no question that some in Ford's management ranks realized that a radical change was required. A change in business practices entailed a change in financial-control orientation. Managing-by-the-numbers had somehow evolved to the point of managing the numbers rather than managing the product with the aid of numbers. Finance had progressively distanced and alienated itself from the people who designed and made the product, as well as the product itself. As a result, the finance function was managing resources, but this process was not contributing to the long-term competitiveness of the firm. Numbers had crowded out the product. The confrontational style of finance staff had reinforced and compounded the dysfunctionality of the confrontational management style that characterized Ford since its most early days.

A New Orientation and New Configuration of Financial Work

Given its strong internal culture and sense of fraternity, as well as its success in feeding the ranks of general management, finance staff assumed that their perspective was the best one for Ford. What the economic crisis spurred (and the Mazda studies made unequivocal) was the need for a shift in the power and role of the financial organization. That shift involved a fundamental change in the posture of the financial organization, from scorekeeping and surveillance over the line units to involvement with and service to the line units. This shift was noted by the current CFO in his discussion of the competitive-team orientation:

> And so, we're therefore driven very much by being a service organization, need I say so much less so today a gatekeeper. We're not a scorekeeper so much. We obviously have to keep score. We have to maintain the company's financial records and report on our financial results. But the emphasis really is on providing a service and being a business consultant to line management, to the operations, rather than trying to second guess them and trying to review and critique what their doing—joining in as a member of the team very early on.

In discussing the change of orientation, a plant-level controller who was at one time involved in the pilot effort at the Hermisillo plant, put it this way:

> . . . a definite change; when I hired in, it was pretty well-known if you were on Lundy's team, you were a step ahead. Finance at that time really sat back and directed a lot more than they do today. Today, we're more service [oriented], at least at plant level.

> [I function] more as an advisor than as the dictator that I might have been a few years ago. Allegiance to the plant versus the finance division level has not been a big problem.

As these quotes imply, the shift to the team orientation has been marked. The shift has entailed a change in the dominant mindset of the finance staff from oversight and enforcement to service and involvement. As the CFO put it:

> The primary emphasis is service to the customer—it is the primary driver for what we do. In order to deliver quality products to customers we have to have teamwork. There were going to be fewer of us around. We did not have as many people . . . we've got to be members of the team. We don't have time. We don't have any excesses or redundancy; we've got to all pull together . . . It's back simply to the marketplace. Finance is no different than any other organization in this company today in that drive. We've all got to do the same thing.

Another interviewee noted that finance staff was "much less of a pure policeman." As the statement of the CFO suggests, the command-and-control orientation entailed oversight and enforcement costs that Ford could not afford. As indicated in the citations from the Finance

Business Plan, as well as in previous quotes, the shift to the team orientation is having a direct impact on the investment in and pattern of financial work. In particular, two points are worth mentioning:

1) The shift from after-the-fact, internally directed review and monitoring to "upstream" analysis can help shape the competitive business decision and, therefore, the bottom line of the company, and

2) The streamlining of accounting and control systems are made possible by the shift to a philosophy of teamwork and employee involvement.

The citations from the Business Plan provide direct evidence of the specific actions and reallocation of resources that Ford has undertaken in the attempt to redirect its energies from oversight to analysis. While this has largely been a finance function initiative, operating people are receptive. As Ken Coates put it:

> Operating people realized that real progress is to be made at the front end of the process. It is now very clear to them that it is where the company has process problems. Decisions aren't clear enough, complete enough, consistent enough. [This] shows up as a whole slew of problems at the downstream end.

Team playing manifests itself in more ways than simply de-emphasizing downstream review and enhancing upstream analysis. The flow of communication in the finance function has shifted from a vertical flow up through the finance function to the CFO, to a horizontal flow, in which divisional controllers focus on serving their line managers rather than the top down review process. This shift has occurred in part because of a shift in the criteria by which finance staff are evaluated and because of the greater input that line managers have in these evaluations.

The shift in the communication flow and organization of the finance function is being implemented right down to the floor of the production plant. As part of the implementation of the innovations tested at the Hermisillo plant, the concept of area management is being implemented within the U.S. automotive plants. Area management is a form of matrix management in which all previously centralized plant-level staff functions are dispersed onto the production floor under the direction of area production managers. Thus, cost analysts—who in the past worked out of a central office under the direction of the plant controller—now live on the production floor and report in a matrix fashion to both the plant controller and the area production manager. This change is part and parcel of Ford's effort to implement the teamwork and employee involvement concepts.

Another graphic example of the team concept, as applied to Ford's focus on quality and serving the customer, was provided by Ron Forsburg, the Controller of the stamping plant in Wayne, Michigan. Ron indicated that his responsibilities include more than traditional financial tasks. He is now responsible for resolving all manufacturing quality problems related to locks, mechanisms and windows, and spends up to a half-day a week on quality issues.

In regard to streamlining the accounting and control systems, we have commented previously on the 40 percent downsizing of the finance staff since 1979 in response to the competitive threat from Japanese automakers. Likewise, we have discussed the significant role that the Mazda studies have played in providing Ford's financial management with concrete evidence of a better way of doing business. Ford has learned that confrontation and distrust are not good business. The presumption that line people are cost drains that need to be plugged, or robbers that have to be monitored and policed by finance staff, has proved to be a losing proposition. A mindset of confrontation and distrust is not only a bad strategy for cost control, it also increases the costs of controlling costs. One interviewee talked about the phenomenon of "controllers controlling the controllers," which leads to duplication and wasted effort that is competitively disadvantageous in today's global marketplace:

> We [now] accept their [purchasing function] controls. In the old days we put controls on their controls because we didn't trust them. That's just wasted effort. It leads to a mass confusion of data—different numbers in different systems.

Dan Coulson, Corporate Director of Accounting, indicated that the team-oriented approach resolves staffing redundancy by locating responsibility for cost control with the business unit performing the work, rather than with the financial function. To effect these economies, the financial organization is shedding its historical surveillance responsibilities and redundant checking:

> Mr. Coulson: We're passing some of the responsibility out to other organizations, which is where we think it belongs in the first place. And they agree, and we're not giving it to them reluctantly. There's mutual agreement. Now material control people have to be absolutely dead sure they received the material they said they received.
>
> Interviewer: Because no one's looking over their [shoulder]?
>
> Mr. Coulson: That's right.

Certainly, the cost pressures associated with foreign competition are a significant motivation behind the drive to simplify and streamline financial operations at Ford. And, what Ford learned through the Mazda studies has contributed in significant measure to making the shift toward a team-oriented operating philosophy. But there is more to what Ford learned from Mazda.

The Philosophy of Continuous Improvement

The Mazda studies have stimulated Ford's finance staff to question the cost effectiveness of financial work practices that had previously been taken for granted as the most appropriate, if not only, way of doing business. The Mazda studies have unfrozen highly institutionalized work practices and set in motion an ongoing process of challenging accepted, time-honored, organizational relations and patterns of financial work. Ford staff refer to this mindset of questioning what has been taken for granted as a philosophy of continuous improvement. In referring to the impact of the Mazda studies, Dan Coulson put it this way:

> Mr. Coulson: It affected [the] accounting group in many many ways. In a broad way, it forced us to rethink how we do our accounting from a transactional standpoint—really from all standpoints. [It] forced us to make a lot of changes that afterward we've found to be very, very beneficial . . . the principle is that we've gone to a completely different approach to come up with something.
>
> Interviewer: Once you decouple from standard ways of doing things, the possibilities start to occur all over the place.
>
> Mr. Coulson: The light goes on, exactly.

Dan Coulson articulated the broader philosophy under which Ford's accounting people are now operating, having had their eyes opened:

> It is a process-improvement philosophy that you have to apply not only to building cars, but doing accounting, engineering, or anything.
>
> We know we have to improve our quality. We know we have to become more customer oriented. We know we have to reduce our costs. And we know we have to do these things as far forward as the eye can see. It is with that perspective that all of us come to work every single day—and that means everything we're looking at in our accounting.

We're always looking for ways to do it better and more efficiently to satisfy our customer, mostly our internal customer. Because of the environment we're operating in, everything we're doing is challenged on a continuous basis for ourselves.

And the significance of process improvement is not lost on Ford's top management. With efficiency still a major objective of the finance organization and in spite of the significant improvements that have been made to date, the current CFO stressed the importance of process improvement efforts. Process improvements being made in accounting have gotten visibility right up to the Office of the Chief Executive. As Dan Coulson noted with some enthusiasm:

The other part of it is exciting . . . The average finance person views these as mundane, routine things. But in our company it has been tremendously exciting. It has gotten visibility right up to the Office of the Chief Executive. It's one of the most innovative things going on in the administrative parts of the business. And I just wish we could get people involved and aware of the exciting things that are available to do . . . .

Some Unresolved Issues and Tensions

The foregoing discussion should not imply that Ford's transition to the competitive-team orientation has been trouble-free or uniformly successful. First, we have been talking about the transition from command-and-control to competitive-team orientation within the top and middle management ranks. The degree to which the competitive-team philosophy has been internalized throughout all levels of management, and between management and labor, is not clear, and certainly not addressed in this study. As Keith Magee, Assistant Controller for Corporate and North American Analysis, put it:

I'm not convinced cultural change has occurred in the bowels of the organization. Given the organization's size, we have a tough time getting people to [change] strategies, etc.

So, what is changing is that the business perspective of the operating guy is moving up, and finance is relinquishing some of that power and joining the team. That's a cultural change which is taking place in Ford. Is it universal? No . . . the term we use, hunchback controllers, still exists.

A second consideration that bears upon the ultimate success of the transition to a team orientation is Ford's "chimney" problem. Keith Magee put it rather directly:

We've had a chimney problem in Ford for a long time. Talking about teamwork is fine, implementing it is another story.

Due in part to its long-standing tradition of functional specialization going back to Henry Ford's production line, as well as its history of functional confrontation, Ford, not surprisingly, is plagued by a functionalist mindset. The chimney metaphor refers to a variety of ills. As Keith Magee put it in contrasting the operation of Ford's financial function with two other companies:

Biggest differences are cultural. Other firms have better team-oriented processes. People have shared objectives; they work closely together . . . [but] their analytic systems are no better than ours. We describe our functional orientations as chimneys. We have a harder time getting people in chimneys working together.

Ken Coates used the chimney metaphor to refer to the functional mentality at Ford:

Units of this business are not SBUs; they are functional lines of organization. Functional organizations have grown here so that they have a life of their own. It is the function that becomes important. Manufacturing people don't think they are part of the Escort team; they think they're part of the manufacturing team—part of the chimney problem. The product line organization is a different sort of chimney. You really want a true matrix.

Mazda, on the other hand, does not have a highly specialized financial organization. Dave Barry, head of Ford's process improvement unit at the time of the interviews, argued that the chimney problem is reflective of a broader societal problem based on an overestimation of the benefits of specialization. The argument is similar to the one made by Piore and Sabel in their book *The Second Industrial Divide*:

That's the dilemma. [Our] overwhelming difference with the Japanese has nothing to do with the Asian culture. It is the fact that they have responsibility at the level at which you can do something about it . . . maybe an engineer is performing a cost-estimating function [in Japan] that by our categorization of people they are called finance . . . many technical people in Japan may be finance types . . . You've got to be careful because there's that case of what I call the specialist in another area. There's the other case of the non-specialist, which is much more germane to the design engineer. The dream of the design engineer is not to make the cost estimator a specialist function within engineering, because we can do that tomorrow; it doesn't make any difference. The issue is really, I designed the car, I should think about the cost. I, me, myself. Not, I design, you cost. There's a distinction in philosophies . . .

And there's a dilemma here with the specialization of function . . . We've all grown up in a world that says, one of the ways the industrial West achieved the huge economies of scale that we did was by specialization of function. We specialize functions. We do not understand, I think, that there's a level of specialization in which communication is a problem and the whole thing just falls apart.

Finally, there are the inherent tensions referred to in an earlier set of quotes, of forging stewardship and teamwork into the same mold. Given their stewardship role as fiscal conscience of the company, finance staff are inherently set off from the team in an important sense. This is the often-cited involvement/independence tension. It is a tension that is managed but never completely resolved. Various prescriptions exist for managing this tension. The interviews reflected this tension. Stan Seneker, the CFO, discussed the challenge that the finance staff faces in constantly establishing themselves as contributing members of the divisional management teams:

Finance, typically because we tend to be viewed as scorekeepers—and I think this probably applies to finance in all businesses—tends to be viewed with a little bit of skepticism by operating people from time to time. So you constantly have to prove yourself—prove yourself to be a member of the team.

Dick Cook argued that in a team-oriented environment, the line manager is a receptive client of financial control:

Stewardship is not a simple tradeoff with team; the stewardship role can be valuable to the operating manager as well.

The CFO noted that if the stewardship needs of the company are to function adequately in a team orientation, the financial person must feel free to go against the grain when the need arises:

The service orientation must be coupled with a climate that encourages open communication so that, when necessary, finance staff feel comfortable speaking up and challenging the client when the need to fulfill the stewardship function arises.

Finally, as committed as he is to a team-oriented financial function, Dave Barry worries about calls for greater upstream involvement in the formulation of business strategy and program proposal development.

Mr. Barry: The other point to make on team playing, which to me is a little risky, is that if there is too much team playing at different levels, one of the tendencies of man is to get very enamored with the projects he's working on. The turn down rate is low, because it is my project, our project. Judgement in the end gets clouded by the fact that I've just spent six months working on this project. It must be good. And there's risk there. There's clear risk there.

Interviewer: Somewhere along the line in any system of check and balance . . . somebody has to be outside that group to ask to the question: Why?

Mr. Barry: Right.

Case Summary and the Conceptual Model

While the transition to a team orientation at Ford is by no means a "done deal," the fact that a transition is in progress cannot be denied. Consistent with our conceptual model, this shift in orientation has been stimulated, in part, by environmental contingency and change, and, in part, by historical contingency. Ford is facing a competitive environment that puts a premium on efficiency and adaptation. This creates a demand for sophisticated financial analysis within a management team context. But as the interview comments point out, the capital-intensive nature of the automotive business has always demanded competent and sophisticated financial analysis. Obviously, this is reflected in the "whiz kid" reputation of Ford's financial function. Sophisticated analysis is not new to Ford. What is new is the shift from distance and distrust to being close to the business and trusting other team members.

Consistent with the conceptual model, and as the qualitative analysis brings out, the shift in orientation at Ford derives as much from historical as economic contingency. The critical events of organizational crisis and the Mazda studies have played a significant role in changing Ford's operating philosophy and financial-function orientation.

Clearly the past orientation of Ford's financial function was that of command-and-control. This orientation followed from the hierarchical and specialized nature of the firm as a whole, and the pervasive climate of conflict and distrust. From a financial viewpoint, the firm was viewed as a bundle of assets to be managed, and employees were viewed as costs to be minimized. As the arm of the Board, finance staff functioned first and foremost as the custodian/trustee and overseer of the company's (and the Ford family's) resources. In this capacity, finance staff's primary source of status and legitimacy was position-based.

As the antithesis of a teamwork orientation, the predominant mindset across the entire company was highly functional, making for the "chimney" mentality mentioned so often in the interviews. This functional orientation also contributed to the confrontational dynamics between finance and line management. The finance organization enforced the internally focused rules established for the allocation and use of the company's assets.

As steward of the Ford family/company assets, the predominant service of the financial organization was monitoring and control. Highly redundant financial control systems were put into place to monitor production processes. The power to veto capital budget requests gave finance staff control over the future direction of the company.

Since the days of economic crisis in the early '80s, Ford has made a dramatic shift to the competitive-team orientation. The role of finance staff has shifted from overseer to business advisor/partner. Finance staff is expected to help the firm compete as a team in an increasingly complex and hostile environment.

The teamwork ethic or orientation is defined, first and foremost, in terms of customer service. Everyone has their customer, including the finance organization. The legitimacy of the financial function now resides primarily in the value of its expertise in helping line management compete effectively.

2

Merck

For the last three years, Merck has been voted America's most-admired corporation in *Fortune Magazine's* annual survey of corporate executives. And within Merck, the financial organization has been rated as the top corporate staff function. Financial professionals are full members of management teams at all corporate and business unit levels. They provide analytic support to the business units while maintaining the integrity of the corporate financial reporting system.

The story of Merck's financial organization is one of change from a moderate command-and-control orientation to a strong competitive-team orientation. We have positioned the Merck story between the Ford and Citicorp stories to emphasize 1) the movement away from command-and-control—the Ford experience—and 2) the movement toward a people-oriented competitive-team orientation—the Citicorp experience. Both qualitatively and quantitatively (based on the distribution of interview comments within the framework of the conceptual model), Merck and Citicorp are the most similar of the six firms in the study. Each financial organization has developed a cadre of financial professionals that are expected to make personal, value-added contributions to the success of the firm. The credibility of these financial professionals rests on their expertise rather than their position within the firm.

Merck's strength in the pharmaceutical field is based on the ability of its researchers and scientists to come up with new ethical drugs that meet a market demand. The financial organization has adopted this research spirit and thinks in terms of developing innovative financial products and practices. The financial organization has demonstrated that it is a solid contributor to Merck's overall success.

The Merck Culture: Leading Edge With a Hard Edge

At Merck, the competitive-team orientation is cast in the language of leading-edge professionalism. The current strategic plan for Merck's financial organization starts with the following mission statement:

> The mission of Merck's financial organization is to improve the Company's profitability through astute financial and tax planning, accounting, reporting, and performance evaluation.

> An important objective is to extend our reputation as one of the most professional and progressive financial staffs in the industry.

> To do this, Merck is committed to achieving excellence in all aspects of its financial organization, with special emphasis on recruiting and developing top-flight individuals.

In itself, the emphasis on developing a leading-edge financial organization is not terribly distinctive. A random selection of financial organization plans would probably turn up many similarly worded statements. What is distinctive about Merck's financial organization is that the rhetoric of leading-edge is underwritten by a very coherent vision that is backed by a strategy for bringing that vision into reality with measurable results.

The CFO, Frank Spiegel, is committed to developing team-oriented financial professionals—professionals who bring sophisticated analytic tools to the decision table and who make substantive contributions to solving management problems. These contributions are based on a solid grounding in the logic of risk and return, and a sound understanding of the business.

Merck hires high-impact individuals from top business schools and provides them with ample resources and an open, flexible work environment. In return, Merck's financial executives expect these individuals to develop innovative financial tools and products that produce a measurable impact on the bottom line. Openness and flexibility are essential. Financial executives at Merck, more so than at any of the other four industrial firms studied in this research, stressed their impatience with narrowly defined job responsibilities. Traditional specialist distinctions, such as accounting and finance, and treasury and control, have no place in the current Merck financial management vision.

Given Merck's commitment to measurable results, it is fair to say that leading-edge is not simply a cliche. Financial products and analytic tools are deemed leading-edge only if they have at least one of the following properties:

☐ They result in a measurable improvement in the firm's profitability;

☐ They represent innovative practices, either introduced into the industry by Merck's financial staff or found in only a limited number of firms; or

☐ They represent practices that outside financial experts (found in leading businesses, banks, consulting firms, or universities) have stated to be highly progressive.

As the Vice President of Finance put it:

> Success in the financial organization really depends on being able to demonstrate that you have contributed in some major way to the financial success of the firm.

The CFO was rather direct when it comes to that commitment to making a tangible contribution to the firm's profitability:

> I won't put anything on our list of accomplishments [going to the CEO] that you can't put a buck on.

Apparently, there have been enough successes to report, since the financial organization has received top management's excellence rating more than any other staff organization over the last several years. These successes, along with the shift in financial function orientation from command-and-control to competitive-team, have played an important role in improving the status of the financial organization.

The Shift from Command-and-Control to Competitive-Team

The emphasis on leading-edge financial management belies a shift in posture and position within the firm. Consider the following comments by the Vice President—Research Administration:

> I think there's been a tremendous change in the financial area—probably in the last five to seven years. [Historically] I would look at the financial people and it didn't matter whether we were making drugs or shoes or anything else. Financial people did financial things. They didn't perceive themselves as being part of the company in decision making, even at the top of the company. They didn't consider themselves an integral part of management; at the divisional level they too were divorced.

> The biggest single change I found as of late was their participation in the area that they're involved with . . . more substance and more caring and more trying to understand what it is . . . what the client is about.

These comments are significant in that they come from a top member of the research organization in a firm where research is paramount. The comments are indicative of the basic shift in orientation that has occurred over the past five to seven years, most notably over the last three to four years. The shift has been away from arm's-length monitoring and control to customer (client) service and involvement in the business.

In making this shift, the financial organization has become more influential in shaping competitive decisions. Possibly, the most tangible evidence of the importance of the financial point of view within Merck is the increased involvement and influence of the current CFO, Frank Spiegel, as a member of Merck's top management team, the Operating Review Committee (ORC). Again, the Vice President—Research Administration notes:

> You put your money where your mouth is. Frank's recent promotion says he is more than a financial guy doing a traditional financial role.

> If you look at Frank Spiegel's role in the company today and even his role two to three years ago, it was more than just a financial person. By being part of the management team he not only was a member by designation, but he was a member by doing . . . In our history that was not considered part of their [finance's] job description—it may be a philosophy, it may be the people, it was sort of that's not my area, I shouldn't have to get involved.

The shift in orientation toward greater involvement and influence has not been as dramatic as the shifts found in the financial organizations at AT&T, Citicorp, and Ford. Rather, the shift appears to be one of movement away from a muted command-and-control orientation to a very visible competitive-team orientation. We use the term "muted" for two reasons. First, the interview comments do not surface an historically strong or distinct financial culture at Merck. Certainly, there are clear references in the interview comments to tensions between financial and line management that are indicative of a traditional command-and-control approach to financial control; however, these references are not extensive.

In referring to the previous orientation of the financial organization, one Vice President offered the following comment:

> If you lined up people in every operating area, they'd tell you financial was a big pain in the ass and did stifle things. Whether they did or not, that was the perception.

There were also shades of confrontation and second guessing. A Senior Director—Finance, explained:

> Interviewer: This shift to a service orientation is something divisions see as a definite change?

> Senior Director: Absolutely. You should get the same type of vibes from everybody you talk to. We certainly have changed from lunging forward at people to the point of walking along with them.

On a similar note, he recalled some of the past confrontational style:

> It was a contentious issue. As division controller, I was expected to give the [corporate] controller a list of questions . . . that would expose that "they" [operating divisional management] were asking for too much. The second year I gave a copy to [the controller] and the division head. He [the controller] went into orbit. To me it was the classic culture being established that you were there, but you weren't there to work and smooth things along. [You were] there to say, I wouldn't have done that."

It can be argued, and Merck staff do, that as the environment in the pharmaceutical industry has become more complex and risky, the need for sophisticated financial analysis has increased. It is a well-established fact that the research pipeline was running dry for the entire industry in the 1970s. Financial strategies were needed to ride out the dry years. The dry years also coincided with the repeal across the U.S. of anti-substitution laws (which had effectively outlawed generic drugs). Product sales can now drop by as much as 50 percent in the first year after a drug goes off patent. Merck anticipated more intense competition leading to reduced margins and returns on R&D and capital. This perceived environmental threat was reflected in Merck's 1988 corporate strategic plan (see Corporate Strategic Plan Summary, The Spirit of Global Competition, 1988).

The strategic plan identifies a number of strategic issues and action plans of a directly financial nature, including issues concerned with 1) managing a complex organizational and capital structure stemming from Merck's growth and worldwide marketing and manufacturing presence, 2) managing Merck's stated external growth strategy, and 3) coping with potential regulatory constraints on pricing freedom. On the last issue, Merck is concerned that claims of increasing profits could lead to regulatory restrictions on the freedom of pharmaceutical firms to set product prices, thereby reducing economic returns.

In addition to issues of environmental complexity, managing growth, and responding to increased regulatory pressure, two specific changes initiated by the financial organization have played an important part in the shift to a competitive-team orientation.

Key Financial Organization Initiatives

Merck's current CEO, Dr. Roy Vagelos, believes in having a strong measurement-based performance evaluation system. And the current CFO, Frank Spiegel, has been intimately involved in developing and integrating a new Merck measurement-oriented culture. Two initiatives are particularly significant in this regard:

1) Merck made its divisional managers full resource managers and the financial organization supported the move by developing a comprehensive ROA-based measurement and performance evaluation system.

2) The financial organization also developed an R&D planning model to improve the strategic management of Merck's substantial R&D investment process.

Through its success in these two ventures, the financial organization has demonstrated its commitment to a competitive-team concept, and has demonstrated that it can make a measurable difference in the financial performance of the firm. The financial organization is now involved in business decision making to an extent unequalled in its recent past. As earlier comments indicate, the value of the financial organization's stock and its status within the firm have risen substantially.

The ROA-based Performance Evaluation System

In the early 1980s, Merck was experiencing, by its own historical standards, underpar profit margins, asset turnover, and return on assets (ROA). Merck had fallen into the bottom half of the pack compared to the other twelve leading pharmaceutical companies.

One of the reasons for the improvement in financial performance since that time can be traced to the ultimately very wise decision to continue to invest heavily in R&D. Merck is now reaping the rewards from that investment. The lower (by pharmaceutical industry standards) profit margins, asset turnover, and ROA reflected the lag between making the investment decision and realizing the benefits of the investment through increased sales. In retrospect, the investment in R&D paid off; however, at the time, risks were taken with only a hope for the return.

Frank Spiegel talked about the contribution of the financial organization during this period:

> When we turned the corner into the 1980s, what is normal in this high risk business set in: we had a dearth of products and we had dollars going the wrong way . . . our returns were going in the wrong direction and our cost of capital was going in a counter direction.

> So we had to change the culture to get people thinking about asset management. . . The changes that we've made in a couple of years are absolutely unbelievable in terms of redirecting assets. At a strategic meeting in 1982, I introduced a couple of concepts about return when I was in the planning function . . . that bit into the system.

> Then we moved it into the annual measurement system. So it has really bitten. And people are now full resource managers, as opposed to being quasi-marketing people.

> So there's a big drive if you have an asset that is not making its cost of capital and is never expected to, to do something different with that resource.

> My guess is that our success story in the last three years is better than anything you read in the papers about other company restructuring programs.

In terms of ROA, Merck has moved from the bottom half into the upper quartile of the twelve leading pharmaceutical companies. Merck is now shooting for the number one rank. As Merck has improved its ROA, the market has responded with a substantially appreciated stock price. Merck has successfully integrated traditional financial measures into its management performance evaluation system. The financial organization provides valuable support service to the line managers who are responsible for achieving their business objectives. Management is now measured, and expected to outperform, in several distinct financial comparisons. Up to 70 percent of a division's management bonus is based on these financial comparisons outperforming selected top-line competitors. Another 15 percent is associated with proven continued improvement versus last year, and a final 15 percent is based on performance against the current plan. The financial measures, and divisional response to achieving and exceeding them, have contributed substantially to fully integrated divisional and company financial targets and provide objective management performance evaluations.

The R&D Planning Model

Merck's financial organization has also made a major, innovative contribution to improving the sophistication of the R&D planning process. In addition to implementing a fully-integrated ROA-based performance evaluation system, the financial organization has developed an extremely sophisticated R&D planning model that introduces a financial discipline into the R&D planning process. The researchers and scientists at Merck are among the company's most important assets. The management challenge is to maintain and improve the productivity of the investment in R&D. The financial organization has translated this challenge into the development of the R&D planning model. The R&D planning model will be discussed more fully later in the Merck story.

It could be argued that adding analytic sophistication to the strategic management of Merck's R&D programs was a natural extension of the strong measurement-oriented culture of the R&D group. Yet, the financial staff members who initiated the project faced the same skepticism any outsider faces in coming into an organization under the pretense of providing help. Within the operating divisions of many American corporations, fear of Trojan horses—not to say corporate spies—runs deep. At Merck, performance must precede legitimacy and credibility.

As it turns out, the head of the R&D division at the time the R&D planning model was being developed was Dr. Vagelos, the current CEO. Dr. Vagelos' support was critical to overcoming the fears among the research staff that members of the financial organization were intruding.

The Influence of the CEO

The interview comments indicate that there has always been a long-standing relationship between the CEO and the financial organization at Merck. The Vice President—Controller commented on the current, centralized financial organization:

We are highly centralized. We were that way the day I started with this company. A lot of this follows the philosophies of your CEO. One former CEO, Henry Gadsen, was a very control-conscious guy. He wanted to know what was going on everywhere. If you want that kind of information in that kind of depth, you can't have a decentralized organization—even within your own function of a controller . . . you'd go out and get nothing but noise . . . It got extremely difficult for people to pull together data without a lot of grief and argument and convincing that that's what you wanted. Gadsen changed the reporting relationship.

The other driving force you have here is: what does your Chairman think of your financial area? Does he want the information . . . Gadsen was a strong user of financial data and wanted a lot of detail. Vagelos uses these data to measure their (managers') performance. In his first year in the company, he, along with his CFO, stressed the philosophy that we are going to enhance stockholder value—through growth and profitability—and divisions are measured by it. That enforces the financial role.

While there is some difference of opinion within the financial organization about the strength of the commitment of previous CEOs for the financial organization, Dr. Vagelos is a particularly strong advocate and supporter of financial management. As a noted research scientist, he comes from a culture of measurement and numerical analysis. Judy Lewent, who served as Controller of Merck's Research Division when Dr. Vagelos headed that unit, explained the impact that a single individual can have on a financial organization:

The influence of the financial function has dramatically accelerated over the last three years because of Vagelos' support, insight, and understanding; and hopefully what [we] did for all those years when he was listening for the first time to the financial people . . .

Referring to the changes in the company's size and environment, Ms. Lewent remarked:

Roy [the CEO] has a willingness to accept change and we have a responsibility to figure out how to do it right, and be a contributor instead of a ball and chain on the operating divisions and research division to get the job done. If we prove our value, we'll get the resources we need and have an exciting environment, attract good people and do the job we need to do.

The Vice President—Controller spoke also of Vagelos' personal Executive Information System (EIS) and the increase in financial assessments of the firm's performance:

[The EIS reports on] the performance of every market in the world—plan vs. actual vs. prior year, plus a graphic display of products—providing a series of fifty charts. Vagelos accesses [the EIS] regularly. He has used it to call up and question divisional heads. He is a strong user of financial information.

[Regarding business forecasting,] It is a very big thing with Vagelos. We've imposed forecasting on top of our total reporting system. Because at mid-year, he wants to reassess where he's going . . . I give the presentations to the ORC [Operating Review Committee] . . . we do a risk analysis . . . and Vagelos will ask, "How confident are you in this?" . . . [and in responding to this query] I've accepted a responsibility.

"I've accepted responsibility." Merck's culture of leading-edge professionalism that underpins the competitive-team orientation is a very people-centered management philosophy. At Merck, terms such as personal contribution, individual expertise, training and development replace terms such as task, specialization, and function that pervade the interviews at some of the other firms in the study. This culture of leading-edge professionalism is described in the next section.

The Heart of the Competitive-Team Orientation: Participation, Sophistication, and Communication

The Vice President—Controller's comment embodies the core elements of the competitive-team orientation at Merck. First, the Controller's role in the mid-year assessment is not a passive one of simple number crunching. The Controller is a key participant in the management process and he is expected to exercise his business judgement, for which he is accountable. Second, members of the financial organization are expected to perform comprehensive and sophisticated analyses of business problems using the logic of risk/return, informed by a thorough understanding of the business. Finally, the communicative aspect of financial analysis is every bit as important as the sophistication underpinning the conclusions. The financial professionals within Merck are expected to make positive contributions to business decisions by being analytically sophisticated, communicatively competent, and accountable for their recommendations.

The credibility of the financial organization is defined not only in terms of expertise and competence, but trust and communication as well. Sophisticated analysis that befuddles or back bites, that fails to address the issues or support the communicative process, is not credible. To be successful, sophisticated analysis must support the communicative process of the management team, and the financial professionals are held accountable for the quality of the analysis. They are no longer impartial, third-party commentators on the successes and failures of other members of the organization.

The team metaphor at Merck is an explicit one. The CFO stressed the team orientation at Merck as the starting point for fulfilling corporate financial-control responsibilities:

> I think it is more the whole team atmosphere [as opposed to checks and balances]. We're all pulling oars in same direction.

In Merck, being a member of the team means that the financial organization must bring more than a financial perspective to the decision table. To have credibility, financial professionals must:

1) Bring a distinctive competence and business perspective to the decision-making process that can make a difference in the decision outcome, and

2) Effectively manage the joint imperatives of corporate accountability and participation as part of the divisional unit team. This latter requirement is especially challenging in Merck because divisional controllers report on a solid-line basis to the Corporate Controller, not to the divisional unit managers.

Financial professionals must manage this tension by building credibility based on expertise, not position. The stewardship role is an important and necessary one, but taking a stand on control issues, when necessary, should be based on credibility founded on competence, not fear based on position within the organization. Quoting from one senior financial officer:

> My view of the divisional controllers is that they should be considered confidants and membeFrs of the team, not selling their soul, but respected for their credentials and their judgement. Credibility built on expertise permits you to take a stand on controls . . . without being perceived as a policeman . . . If you have respect in your business acumen, and they know you have concern for corporate assets, there can be mutual respect.

At Merck, the distinct competence that the financial person brings to the decision-making table is the logic of risk and return. The framework of risk/return and the array of decision-making tools grounded in risk/return logic provide a basis for disciplining the decision-making process and improving communication among members of the management team. In commenting on the recent criticisms of "managing-by-the-numbers," the Vice President—Treasurer discussed her image of the finance person:

[This gets to my] vision of a finance person—and I don't believe it is a bean-counter and a policeman . . the superficial attack on finance not being receptive to modern technology and to modern management and to short sightedness is also a lot of bunk . . . [following principles of finance such as returning the cost of capital, factoring in uncertainty and risk] doesn't mean. . . that you sit there in the financial area and say, No, you can't do that . . . In fact, I think economics and finance are very enlightened. We've been working quite a bit on the use of option theory and Monte Carlo analysis to enlighten [management] about what risk is, and what acceptable ranges are. We do not say that you have to make this number or we won't take this project.

The language of risk/return was used extensively throughout the interview comments. The Vice President—Controller also made reference to the divisional controller as an evaluator of business risk:

My people have got to step into the business. I want them to tell me how confident they are in it . . . they should know what's going on in that business. And they should know where the exposures are. And we ask them to do a risk analysis. We ask them at profit plan time . . . where are the major risks with this plan? . . . All of this is based on analysis, on their knowledge of the markets, what kind of introductions we have, what kind of market share do they have in those markets . . . Then we come down to what we call a confidence kind of schedule. Do we think we can achieve this for the year?

Most of my people today have an excellent reporting relationship with their divisions . . . the idea is to put together the risks on [the division's] behalf . . . put the risks on the table. . . all this is good intelligence and input into Vagelos . . . It's just a vehicle "to get it up on table."

The financial organization contributes to the management team by insuring that all aspects of the business problem are "put on the table" and analyzed within the framework of risk and return. "Putting the risks on the table" aptly characterizes the qualities of participation, competence, and communication that are expected from the financial professionals within Merck.

At this stage in the story, we will return to a more complete discussion of the "R&D planning model" to expand on the logic of risk/return and show how the financial professionals contribute in a measurable way to Merck's success.

The R&D Planning Model: An Exemplar of Leading-Edge Financial Work

The concepts behind the R&D planning model are not new; Merck has always thought in terms of ten- to twenty-year planning horizons. What is new is the actual, operational, computer-based planning model. The financial organization has developed and implemented the planning model to support management, not second guess their decisions. The R&D planning model provides management with a tool to explore alternatives with greater sophistication and in greater detail than has been possible in the past. The decisions made with the help of the model are then integrated into Merck's capital budgeting process.

As a project that he has championed, Frank Spiegel extols the model's virtue, and the professional and technological sophistication required to make the model a reality:

> We have a planning model that is the envy of any company in the world. It is become a living document that's part of the total planning system and in resource allocations in research. We couldn't have done that without getting the people and the technology.

The model contributes more to the decision-making process than just analytic sophistication. As the Vice President—Research Administration hastens to emphasize, the model is seldom used to make go/no go decisions with respect to particular research programs. Rather, the principal value of the model lies in improving communications among all the members of the management team. The productivity of an R&D program is dependent upon a complex array of factors. Just understanding what all these factors are and communicating this information to individuals from marketing, R&D, and manufacturing is no small challenge. Judy Lewent, who led the development of the model, argues that the model has provided a common set of terms and a common foundation upon which the communicative process at Merck has now been built. The model offers a comprehensive framework for understanding all of the interrelationships that must be managed. The model is where all the numbers have to come together, even when people do not agree about the implications of the numbers.

In the following interchange on the topic of the R&D model, Ms. Lewent reiterated the more general communicative function of finance:

> Ms. Lewent: It [the model] is the only thing they will agree on . . . the numbers. That is the only thing that has caused a truce. They all accept that. They gave input. We've had consensus time after time.

Interviewer: The model serves as an intermediary . . .

Ms. Lewent: I think finance does that everywhere.

The Vice President—Research Administration confirmed the value of the model in supporting the communications process:

> . . . That's true, that's fair. In this way . . . at least we're all speaking the same language . . . the other thing is that we are putting [things] in the same frame of reference . . . forcing definitional issues . . . It does structure that relationship [of research with marketing]. So we both know we're talking about the same thing. It forces everyone to think a little more, to commit. Those are the major gains of the model.

The success of the R&D planning model has demonstrated the value-adding potential of the financial organization in the management of the research enterprise. The model exemplifies the vision that the CFO is attempting to implement: servicing the internal business customer and being a partner in the decision making process through knowledge of the business and through the application of innovative financial tools that help frame decisions and facilitate communication.

Clearly then, the team orientation at Merck, as articulated in the preceding analysis and as exemplified in the R&D planning model, represents a distinct operating philosophy and pattern of relationships with other organizational units.

Building a Leading Edge Financial Organization: The Human Resource Strategy

A revealing aspect of Merck's commitment to being a leading-edge financial organization is evidenced by its expenditures per employee in the area of financial planning and analysis. While Merck had the lowest ratio of financial function costs to company sales of all the pharmaceutical firms that reported this figure in a recent study conducted by the Pharmaceutical Manufacturer's Association in 1987, it had the second highest cost per financial employee in the financial planning and analysis area. This latter figure is consistent with Merck's strategy for building a leading-edge organization: namely, investing in high-impact individuals who possess the skills and talent to produce financial innovations that enhance the profitability of the firm. As the Vice President of Finance put it:

> We want to go out and find really bright people to do these things. That's where true productivity increases come from. Getting good people gives you good hit-

ting power . . . We're trying to get more of those people built into our organization and challenge them.

Merck's strategy is to hire individuals with the drive and capacity to do leading-edge financial work. Management's responsibility is to establish a professional environment that explicitly values and encourages creative behavior. Then, given the resources, tools, and technology to support these individuals, top management expects a financial chemistry to take place similar to the chemistry that occurs in the research labs.

Another revealing indication of Merck's commitment to investing in top-notch individuals is that Merck establishes a target for the amount of training that each staff person must undertake. In calculating year-end management incentive compensation, a certain amount of bonus points are given to those managers who reach the floor for training and development. Additional bonus points are awarded up to a ceiling. Between 1986 and 1987, the financial organization significantly increased its budget for training and development by over 20 percent.

To complement its professional development strategy, Merck is attempting to establish a climate of challenge and creativity. As Judy Lewent explained, the aim is to:

Get that atmosphere, the bubbling up of ideas, of looking to outside, encouraging a willingness to read; it (the ethic of creativity and innovation) is critical.

But true to the hard edge on Merck's leading-edge culture, the atmosphere is only a means to a very concrete desired end, namely the creation of specific innovations that impact the bottom line. Financial innovation is defined as either:

1) The development of financial tools and analysis that help give answers to business questions and stimulate management actions that get the right financial results, or

2) The development of financial products that directly impact the bottom line.

Merck's financial executives point to a whole laundry list of financial products that have increased cash flows, such as the exploitation of the safe harbor leasing regulations and use of option theory to restructure executive stock options. Thus, Merck's financial organization assesses its own performance in terms of its success in creating value, not simply maintaining the value created by other organizational units.

Financial innovations are the work of stimulated individuals and teams of financial professionals. As a staff person you are given the resources and moral support to perform, but you are evaluated on the basis of the measurable difference that you make. In the following comment, the Vice President and Treasurer reinforced the financial organization's penchant for innovation that is on a par with their peers in research and manufacturing:

> You don't get a good rating for doing your job . . . You get a good rating by doing something way beyond your job. Something really tangible, something new.

Interview comments also stressed the vision for a culture of financial professionalism. As the CFO, put it:

> My three words are creativity, challenge, and professionalism. Professionalism wraps everything up as far as I am concerned . . . it gets you into doing your own R&D, into increasing your training and development programs internally, and into going outside to interact with knowledgeable professionals.
>
> Interviewer: The management philosophy is more cultural than structural . . .
>
> No two ways about it—lean and in front of our competition technologically. That's what we're trying to do with people and technology.

In the next section, we discuss the key financial organization strategies for designing a culture of leading-edge professionalism.

Some Key Design Strategies

In addition to strong recruiting and development policies, and efforts to foster professionalism, there are three explicit organizational strategies that figure centrally into Merck's overall leading-edge posture:

1) An emphasis on financial research and development that complements the strong scientific R&D culture at Merck;

2) Management leadership that attempts to provide focus for financial innovations through a strong issues orientation tied to the competitive and financial strategy of the firm; and

3) The breakdown of traditional boundaries between treasury and control roles within the financial function. The evolution of a new role model: that of financial advisor capable of integrating the traditional disciplines of tax, financial analysis, and control.

Emphasis on Financial R&D

In discussing the functions of the financial organization, the Vice President of Finance identified three broad sets of activities that are analogous to those of a complete business: the production shop (financial operations), the marketing effort (corporate and divisional controllers), and the R&D function. He referred to the latter as the function that is at the heart of the change in the financial organization:

> The third function of finance is analogous to R&D. It is new product development within the finance function . . . the thinking side of the finance function in terms of what's going on now, where we should be going strategically, how we are going to get there . . . There's no central core of staff set aside for this . . . this is really the challenge and the thing that's changing, and the future of the financial function.

This notion of financial R&D was touched upon in other interviews. Frank Spiegel referred to the notion of financial R&D within the context of his vision of a leading-edge financial organization:

> . . . Excellence in finance, recruiting, challenge, creativity, communications, and training and development; I really think those are six key things, all under this professionalism, which really says that you've got to do your own R&D, have some training; that you've got to really stay out in front of all the literature and be searching for new products and that kind of thing.

As noted earlier, the R&D function is not specific to an organizational unit, but rather is an attitude to be adopted by everyone within the organization. Innovation is supposed to be part and parcel of everyone's job. Frank Spiegel elaborated on the creation of an atmosphere conducive to learning and innovation:

> So I see people, technology, issues, analysis as really [the key]; challenge and creativity, too. We're trying to create an atmosphere where you do not get your head handed to you. Challenge is another big piece of it. It is a mindset. Issue management is a mindset.

The research mindset is reflected in specific programs within Merck's financial organization. For instance, the financial organization has undertaken a series of institutional studies to address the issue raised by regulators regarding profits in the ethical pharmaceutical drug industry. This effort also includes the development of a retrospective model that examines the historical financial performance of new compounds introduced in the past. The model documents the risk involved and the historical reliance of the industry on a relatively few "blockbuster" products that carry the majority of the other products that do not earn back their cost of capital.

As a second example, staff members are encouraged to use outside consultants to stay apprised of new financial products and to assist with the development of new financial tools. The Vice President and Treasurer described the value she places on access to outside expertise and reaching out as a basic management philosophy:

> I would say that the most important factor beyond good financial systems is access to experts outside this company . . . to know what the new products are, what best pricing is, to know what the competitive environment is outside. Merck is a very small user in a very big system. And if we're going to be cost effective, and really smart, and have the best products, the only way you're going to do that is by constantly reaching out to see what's going on . . . go to conferences to find out what others are doing . . . get out into the world by meeting regularly with investment and commercial bankers to find out what they're doing.

There are also studies underway with faculty at leading universities to examine the use of option theory and to study Merck's real cost of capital in relation to that of Japanese firms. The latter study is part of the effort to address regulatory concerns about industry profits:

> We have a little mini-economics shop trying to do some studies with outside universities to elucidate our point intelligently—hopefully to get enlightenment on the part of regulators and Congressman, the EEC, and Japan.

Emphasis on Issues

To insure that innovative behavior addresses the needs of the business, the entire financial organization operates under a strong issues orientation. All analyses produced by the staff members must be issue-focused. Frank Spiegel, the current CFO, stressed the value of an issue orientation for coalescing management action:

> Once you get through people and technology . . . it is an analysis function and an issue function that really makes the thing work. Good hard analysis, laying out the facts as best you can . . . but then issues. We've identified ten key issues in the company. That's all we want to have. And we rang bells like the Salvation Army making people address issues, to come up with strategic action programs to deal with these issues. And we feel if that's successful, we're going to be successful.

Merck's top financial executives meet routinely to formulate and monitor the strategic direction of the financial organization, including making an assessment of the most fruitful areas for new financial "product development." The CFO also holds monthly strategic-issue sessions. A different issue is addressed at each meeting with different people attending depending on the issue. These sessions have dealt with R&D productivity, asset utilization, capital structure, and manufacturing cost control. The meetings serve as brainstorming sessions that result in new ideas and proposals for product and decision-tool innovation; they foster communication among staff members who might not otherwise come into contact with each other; and they reinforce, in a regular and highly visible way, the strong issue orientation:

> The idea of those strategic issue meetings—they're helpful in getting everyone together and just preparing for them. But then, we run them very wide open so [together] there's a lot of challenge and no bruised egos; we can use it [the meeting] to challenge and to deal with strategic issues, and also to communicate . . . Some neat issues come out of there. It seems to me that is part of the "new product" kind of thing and leading-edge of technology, because that's what we're trying to drive for, staying ahead and trying to tie that into identifying issues that will get us out in front of people.

Breaking Down Boundaries

Finally, in an effort to foster individual initiative while recognizing the need for integrated approaches to problems, Merck's financial management has made an effort to tear down the boundaries associated with traditional jobs and roles within the financial organization (such as treasury and controller, or accounting and finance), while making greater use of individual participation in problem-oriented task forces.

The emphasis on individual initiative consists of job flexibility coupled with a "show me" philosophy of recognition and reward for creating value-adding financial tools and products:

> The culture that I [Vice President and Treasurer] personally take to heart and try to disseminate is that there are no boundaries on your job description, and the only thing I'd ask is for someone to come up with an idea. Anything you want to do we'll do if it is worth doing . . . If you do something, it'll be there. But you've got to get people to understand that the culture is [to] come forward, do things. Don't tell me you don't have resources. Look beyond that, figure that they'll come

if you've added value and there's something worth doing. You'll get them, but you've got to give something first. Maybe that's the research side too. It's sort of test it, show me why it is worth doing, prove yourself, expend a little extra effort if you think it is so good, and in the end you will be rewarded and you'll also get the support.

The elimination of traditional boundaries extends beyond individual job descriptions. Judy Lewent was vociferous about her impatience with the constraints imposed by traditional boundaries ("chimneys" at Ford) within the financial organization:

> I have this very specific view of what a division controller should be. And I see all of it as almost nondifferentiable in function, and I see the financial person as a business partner who happens to have expertise in finance and accounting and so on.

Merck's financial organization is pursuing a variety of approaches to integrate traditionally separate functions. Referring to the importance of integration, Ms. Lewent discussed the issue of career movement:

> A very important strategy [to foster intra-function integration] . . . where it counts most is . . . where you have people who have always been in treasury. They have a treasury view and a bias. People in the controller's area have a controller's bias. And you're not going to get rid of that unless people experience the other side. And there's been a conscious effort, but it is going to take time . . . to move people . . . in a funny sort of way, to dislodge these tree trunks that have been in these areas for years . . .

A very concrete, if not innovative step taken by the current CFO to foster this cross-fertilization has been to create an organizational unit with responsibilities encompassing the traditional boundaries of treasury and control. The individual placed in charge of this unit, called Financial Evaluation and Analysis (FE&A), was given "dual but interlocking responsibilities." These responsibilities include 1) evaluating all capital requests, 2) evaluating business acquisitions and divestitures, and prospective licensing of new products, 3) developing the firm's product cost allocation methodology, and, in addition, 4) have responsibility for the controllership of the two major capital intensive divisions, manufacturing and research. There were multiple objectives involved in the establishment of the FE&A, as the following comment by the current CFO suggests:

> When I came back to the financial area, I created that function [FE&A] to encourage asset utilization and for the economics. And economics came into play because, looking at our strategic plan . . . it was clear . . . we were in for exciting

times to break away from the competition. And the chances of justifying our profits, prices and patents versus anyone else . . . So we had to get our story together.

The day that I came back to the financial area was the day of consolidation, not necessarily the addition, of what I then called Financial Evaluation and Analysis, to give that [analysis] purpose, to give it focus, to let it serve ORC and the Board. The main thing we wanted to do there is get away from the single-bullet type of financial evaluation, and get into a range of possibilities . . . get the issues out so that it wasn't incumbent upon management and the Board of Directors to sift through a ton of papers . . . that's a major difference in the Board's sophistication, I think.

The CFO also used FE&A as a mechanism to signal his intent to break down the traditional boundaries within the financial organization, boundaries that he perceives to be barriers to innovative financial work. Referring to the chimney problem and the CFO's move to create FE&A, the Vice President and Treasurer commented:

The controller's area is on one side, the treasurer's area is on the other and there's an imaginary line there. So [the CFO] said, we're going to solve this. I'm going to give you [FE&A] to force communication.

In the following interchange, Frank Spiegel confirmed this commitment to FE&A as a signal of his desire for his staff members to begin to think beyond traditional intra-function boundaries:

Mr. Spiegel: FE&A, incidentally, was just the conglomeration of various departments. That drove the [divisional] controllers crazy because in their mind financial services for manufacturing should be with the controller. I now have it in treasury.

Interviewer: You're trying to break down those distinctions rather than reinforce them.

Mr. Spiegel: Someday I would like to get away from even having controllers and treasurers. There's something else. I mean something completely wild, as long as its effective.

FE&A has served as a vehicle to implement two key organizational changes:

1) The development of issues-oriented, sophisticated, financial analysis that

2) Cuts across the disciplinary boundaries of finance and accounting traditionally found within the financial organization.

Hopefully, the foregoing analysis of the interview comments has conveyed the soft as well as the very hard edge of the culture within Merck's financial organization. Hopefully, as well, we have shown how Merck's financial organization represents an embodiment of the competitive-team orientation as that concept has been developed in this study. Consistent with the notion that each firm has its own conception of the competitive-team orientation, as a function of its history and the unique contingencies it currently faces, we have seen that Merck's competitive-team orientation has shades of similarity and difference in relation to the competitive-team orientations articulated in the other cases.

Case Summary and the Conceptual Model

The foregoing analysis suggests a shift within Merck's financial organization from a muted command-and-control orientation to a prominent team orientation. Consistent with our conceptual model, this shift in orientation has been stimulated, in part, by a business environment that is becoming increasingly more complex and strategically risky. But the business environment is not the whole story. Given its R&D culture and predisposition to measurement, modeling, and analysis, Merck's top management is quite receptive to having a financial organization that emphasizes sophisticated analysis in support of management.

The shift in orientation to competitive-team has been spearheaded by the CFO, Frank Spiegel, and his staff. They have been extremely successful in "selling" the services of the financial organization and demonstrating the value of the financial organization to a new CEO that has a strong measurement and numbers orientation.

As noted in the analysis, the past orientation appears to have been that of muted command-and-control. Although the data collected in this study do not provide extensive evidence in this regard, some interview comments do indicate a financial organization that emphasized oversight and arm's-length interaction versus partnership and service to line management. A final comment from the interviews is timely with regard to the change in orientation. The Vice President—Research Administration remarked:

But it all goes around the fact that you either have participating financial [staff], or you have third-party auditors or CPAs that tell you, Yep, you just spent too much. That's what happens so often. Now the financial organization is an integral part of decision making and strategy of the firm . . . And to me that's a tremendous difference.

The teamwork orientation of Merck's financial organization is most clearly evident in its commitment to be a knowledgeable partner in the decision-making process, and its commitment to adding value to the firm on the basis of its expertise.

3
Citicorp

The financial organization at Citicorp has made a dramatic shift in orientation over the past decade. Under the direction of Tom Jones, the Corporate Officer in charge of Financial Control, the financial control professionals are considered to be valuable members of the management teams throughout Citicorp. The Citicorp story is a good example of the steps a financial organization has to take to move away from being considered "green-eyeshade accountants" to being considered financial professionals. The Citicorp story describes the movement away from a conformance orientation to a competitive-team orientation. Although conformance with external rules and regulations is still an important consideration for any financial institution, it does not have to represent the predominant mindset of the professionals within the organization. The predominant mindset of the financial control group within Citicorp is competitive-team. For organizations faced with the challenges of shifting from a regulated environment to a deregulated (or less regulated) environment, the Citicorp story has much to offer. Changes cannot be made on a piecemeal basis. Citicorp orchestrated a full set of movements that came together to make a harmonious transition in orientation.

Citicorp is a highly decentralized organization and this decentralized approach carries through to the financial function. In addition, there is no question that Citicorp is a firm that is "managed by the numbers." In any organization there is always the danger that a strong numbers orientation can dominate and subvert the business of managing the product and serving the customer. At Citicorp this danger is mitigated by the strong team orientation in which the financial control professionals are highly involved in business operations and decision making. This high involvement strategy results in a healthy blend of active involvement in business decision making while maintaining the integrity of the corporate financial reporting system.

Based on the issues and themes that emerged from the management interviews at all six firms, we would argue that Citicorp's particular brand of competitive-team orientation is most similar to Merck's, although there are important differences, as we should expect. Both Merck and Citicorp have a strong measurement culture, but their cultures allow for and encourage individual initiative and personal contribution. The Citicorp story represents a blending of numbers and people, with the emphasis being on people.

The Shift from a Conformance to a Competitive-Team Orientation

The current financial control philosophy at Citicorp is largely a result of the previous CEO's (Walter Wriston's) belief that Citicorp needed a stronger and more sophisticated financial control function to meet the business challenges of the 1980s. The current CEO, John Reed, has followed Wriston's lead by stressing the need for sound financial controls and giving financial control high visibility throughout Citicorp. At Citicorp, treasury and control report directly to the CEO and not to a CFO. The CFO position does not exist at Citicorp. According to Tom Jones, the Senior Corporate Officer for Financial Control and a former controller at ITT under Harold Geneen:

> The strategic plan is very simple and carefully crafted. Organizationally, we say that control is too important to be part of a classic CFO function. We have Jones who runs accounting, control, MIS, and tax, and Nancy Newcomb who runs funding, capital planning, treasury, etc. Both functions report separately to Reed.
>
> In point of fact, control is quite separate and the reason for that is it would not have the same credibility with the business people if Citicorp had the classic controller structure where the controller reported to a CFO, who reported to the boss. Around here we would be dead. At IT&T, the controller also reported to the CEO.
>
> To Reed, control is very, very important. Control issues are right at the top level of management.

The concern for financial control on the part of the CEO has resulted in a dramatic increase in the level and quality of involvement of the financial control organization in the decision-making process. Financial control staff have moved from being "bean counters" and bookkeepers to being valued team members at both the corporate and business unit levels throughout Citicorp. The dramatic nature of this shift is best captured in the following comment by Tom Jones:

> Ten years ago the term financial control did not exist. We now have the first policy committee member from financial control. When I came, there was an accountant who did consolidations and who did not know who was on the other end. There was also a separate MIS and budget process.

Saleem Muqaddam, former head of Corporate Analysis and Reporting, who has recently made the transition to the business side at Citicorp, made a similar claim in regard to the role of the financial organization at the business unit level:

> Our controllers are the CFOs of the businesses they are in. They have to be part of the senior management team. That is the concept we have.

> There is a clearer recognition of the importance of the role and the function that was not here eight to nine years ago. The group financial controller is a key person in every group. The group consists of profit center managers, division heads, key staff people including the financial person—the CFO role.

At Citicorp, they literally talk about building the current financial control function from scratch. This language is indicative of the dramatic shift that has occurred within the financial function over the past decade. When Walter Wriston took over in 1967, the banking world was changing and Citicorp was moving to become a multiple financial services business: to "provide every financial service that we can, legally and at a profit." Over his twenty-year tenure as CEO, Citibank became Citicorp, a holding company with multiple subsidiaries and diverse kinds of operations. Citicorp became much more like businesses outside of the banking industry. In the 1960s and early 1970s, the financial function provided bookkeeping services oriented toward procedural compliance with regulations promulgated by the bank regulators. According to Tom Jones, before 1970 there was no financial control system per se; the name did not exist:

> . . . In the old days, at the time I'm talking about, you did not need a financial control function, you needed a bookkeeping function because there were few, if any, significant risks. We had an operational manual that was very comprehensive. It dealt with all the things we've learned operating in many countries over 180 years.

. . . Banking had been carefully protected. The rate you paid on deposits was set by law. Only banks could take deposits so there was no competition. There were the usual limits on loans, etc. The accounting in those days was very simple. Every VP had to learn the manuals . . . In this type of environment, why would you need a professional financial function?

As Saleem Muqaddam explained:

We had a mix of people—beancounters, green-eyeshade types and former business managers. Some were financial professionals, others were not. The biggest problem was that we did not have enough strong, independent, talented people to put into the top slots.

As someone who has lived through the transformation of the financial control function, Sean Rogan, current sector Controller for Investment and Institutional Banks, explained:

In the past, financial control was not as professional a control function as we have today. We developed people into experts in legal, tax, regulatory reporting, accounting, budgeting, strategic planning. A financial controller must understand all the businesses in his country or business unit. The thing that has changed is the prominence of the financial function and the relationship of the financial controller to the line manager.

Prior to 1980, financial control did not play an integral role in the management of the business. Accounting and management information were not part of an integrated system. In addition, financial controllers needed to upgrade their skills and position within the organization.

A Move to Decentralization

Before Wriston, financial accounting was relegated to meeting the reporting requirements of bank regulatory agencies and shareholder reporting. As Tom Jones explained:

There were two problems that Wriston perceived because of the dichotomy of views of what the numbers were 1) business managers ran their units on the basis of business numbers generated by a separate reporting system that did not have the discipline of corporate control, and 2) the accounting department reported numbers to the shareholders that came off of a different system. When you compared the two, they were not always the same.

Anyone could attempt to portray the results of their adventures in business in their own way. Once you get enough people explaining their results using their own numbers, not corporate's, you don't know what the truth is. We've stopped this practice and now categorize results more consistently between business units in order to better measure individual contribution.

Also according to Jones, Wriston anticipated that as Citicorp diversified and the banking industry became more deregulated, a highly sophisticated financial control system would be required to support the decentralized management style of Citicorp. Wriston decided that Citicorp needed to hire senior professionals with the know-how and talent required to establish a strong financial control system such as those found at Ford, GE, or IT&T.

In 1980, Tom Jones was hired away from IT&T to more fully integrate the control function into Citicorp's five business segments: Investment Banking, Institutional Banking, the Individual Bank, Insurance, and Information Systems. Second on Jones' list of priorities was the need to establish a reporting system that would produce shareholder and management reporting information from the same underlying accounting records—a single-stream reporting system. This approach to reporting was not implemented prior to Jones' arrival, primarily because the financial organization did not have the resources to initiate a change of this significance. The financial organization, before Jones' arrival, had not yet begun to exert its influence and strength as it would in the coming decade. Tom Jones explained:

> What was perceived to be missing was a budget system and an MIS system based on the financial accounting system that would enable management to understand the business . . . The accountants here at the time did not initiate this change because they did not have the full commitment and support of senior management because, rightly or wrongly, they were perceived to be "green eyeshades" instead of financial professionals.

> We started a function called financial control. We started a single-stream reporting system that brought all the numbers together. We cut out the idea of people having their own reporting. And in fact, when someone tries to "interpret" or recharacterize their results, I have to stop it immediately because that can cause a fatal mistake to take place.

The single-stream reporting system, like Merck's integrated legal entity/market reporting system and 3M's commodity P&L system, does not allow different systems for different purposes. Financial discipline and, ultimately, the integrity and credibility of the financial function lie in having a single, integrated reporting system.

The single-stream system has been an important ingredient in establishing the credibility and relevance of financial control within Citicorp. But the single-stream system is only one ingredient, not the entire recipe. Other critical ingredients have been:

1) The increased integration of financial measures into strategy formulation and management performance evaluation. This trend has been strengthened in recent years by the strong numbers orientation of the current CEO, John Reed, as noted previously.

2) The concerted efforts by the corporation to upgrade the position of the financial controllers in the business units and to recruit highly sophisticated individuals for those upgraded positions.

3) The implementation of a flexible communication and control structure.

Financial Measurement at Citicorp

As Citicorp has shifted from a regulatory to a market environment, financial measurement has become a more important feature of business planning and evaluation. Prior to 1980, management success was determined by the size of the asset base. Given fixed spreads between the deposit rate and the investment rate, the greater the asset base, the greater the total return. With the advent of deregulation, Citicorp has been moving to a more explicit ROE performance evaluation system. Tom Jones argues that the ROE objective is even more real today, especially as Citicorp tries to get more growth in its fee-based versus asset-based business to increase returns and more efficiently utilize scarce capital resources. The steady movement toward an ROE-based performance system is consistent with Citicorp's strong emphasis on "managing-by-the-numbers."

With the increased emphasis given to competitive markets, Citicorp's organizational structure has had to change to meet the needs of the marketplace. The financial control structure has changed to parallel business unit realignments. Over the years, Citicorp has switched back and forth between being organized on a global/geographic basis and a customer basis. From a business perspective, Citicorp's current aim is to integrate its institutional and investment banking operations along geographic lines (OECD countries versus emerging economies).

The Financial Professional at Citicorp: The Culture of Personal Contribution and Value-Added Services

The single-stream system and management profitability reporting (the business unit planning and budgeting systems) are key elements of financial control responsibilities at Citicorp. However, the transition from a conformance to a competitive-team orientation has more to do with people than systems. Citicorp has developed a cadre of topnotch financial professionals who have earned the respect of their business peers through value-added performance. Roger Trupin, Citicorp's recently named Controller, started the Accounting Policy function at Citicorp more than 15 years ago. He stresses the importance of value-added performance in commanding respect from the business managers. As Roger observes:

> It is not enough to be a skilled technician. In order to gain the respect and confidence of the line managers, you have to show that you understand their business, their challenges and needs. You must provide solutions to their problems, without compromising the integrity of Citicorp. They respect a topnotch professional even when you give them some bad news.

While not discounting the leadership role played by Wriston and Reed, the push to develop greater professionalism and sophistication within the financial ranks has been driven by two factors:

1) Increased business complexity and risk, and

2) The need to establish a basis of credibility within the Citicorp culture.

With respect to the first factor, the increased complexity and business risk encountered by Citicorp as a result of diversification and deregulation have increased the demand for financial sophistication. These new, high levels of risk must be managed through 1) better analysis in support of business strategy and product development, and 2) sound control over business operations and financial information integrity.

With respect to the second factor, given the highly entrepreneurial and talent-based organizational culture at Citicorp, professional credibility must be established through expertise and contributions to product team and business decisions. Whereas a financial function that lacks sophistication can survive under a conformance orientation, that same financial function is not viable under a competitive-team orientation.

The strategy at Citicorp has been to invest in financial professionals who possess the technical skills and organizational sophistication required to manage the delicate chemistry of entrepreneurialism and financial discipline essential for organizational success in an increasingly dynamic and risk-filled environment. The professional challenge for the financial organization is to achieve total integration into the business as part of the team, while retaining a functional commitment to maintaining the integrity of the financial reporting system. Of course, this is the traditional tension between involvement and independence; balancing the needs of the parts against the integrity of the whole organization.

Citicorp's culture is well known for being highly entrepreneurial with a great deal of emphasis placed on making contributions through the product/business teams. Individuals are expected to contribute to a team effort. The team-oriented culture at Citicorp has some unique characteristics: it is not family in the sense of a clan, but a true competitive-team in the sense of professional athletes who are valued for their talent. As Loretta Allen, head of the newly formed Financial Risk Advisory Group, put it:

> Citibank lives on competition. Only certain people want to work here. You have to have a certain mindset. Citibank thrives on putting its people in competitive situations.

> You have to be an aggressive, outgoing person. It is a vociferous team. It is not a family, it is a team where everyone is expected to pull their own weight. So it is not family, but a highly competitive team.

A Flexible Communication and Control Structure

Citicorp puts a strong accent on individual contribution in order to foster innovative activity and accountability. Yet, there is a need to have communication among members of the product teams and among the product teams themselves to make the decentralized structure work. The best lines of communication in a decentralized environment are often informal rather than structured.

Citicorp professionals are apt to describe the internal working of the firm in terms of a distinction between a chicken and a lobster. In the world of chickens and lobsters, Citicorp is the lobster. A chicken has a rigid bone structure that tightly defines its internal workings, much like a traditional bureaucracy. The lobster, on the other hand, has a rigid shell, but the organs can move around a little bit. As Tom Jones explained:

> The analogy going around Citicorp that everybody likes is one of chickens and lobsters. We are supposed to be a lobster. A chicken is an animal with structures all inside, so it is very stiff and formal so it keeps the chicken running. A lobster has a shell with the whole inside soft and mushy but the shell holds it together.

> Communication must be instantaneous and not governed by a formal rigid chain of command. To that end, we are trying to get away from an obsession with organizational charts and titles because the corporation that is successful in the future will not be bound by hierarchy, pecking orders, and titles. But on the other hand, you do not want to lose all structure. The challenge is to find the right balance.

In light of these comments, it is not hard to imagine the difficulty the organization faced in changing the focus of the financial organization from a conformance orientation to a competitive-team orientation. To be treated as equal players, the quality of the individuals within financial control had to be upgraded in order to establish their legitimacy and credibility as team members. Financial professionals with the raw talent to measure up to the skill levels of the other members of the team had to be recruited. The financial organization needed to be restructured in order to provide an overarching structure of control, while permitting internal flexibility. The lobster model accommodates entrepreneurial energies and open patterns of communication demanded by a competitive-team culture; the chicken model does not.

Citicorp's overall philosophy of decentralization and entrepreneurialism has been incorporated into the strategy for changing the financial control function. The development of a centralized control function would be totally at odds with the overall Citicorp philosophy. Tom Jones has developed a very person-centered, people-oriented financial control function. This concept of control is consistent with the concepts of individual contribution and professionalism at Citicorp. Tom Jones explained:

> The CEO, John Reed, runs Citicorp by the numbers. John wants to have confidence in the numbers, but John runs a very, very decentralized company. We want to know that in every business we run anywhere in the world there is a person responsible for the integrity of the financial process acceptable to us [corporate] as an individual in order for the matrix reporting relationship to work.

Citicorp invests in individual professionals who possess the technical skills and organizational sophistication required to manage the delicate chemistry of entrepreneurialism and financial discipline essential for success in an increasingly complex, dynamic, and risky environment. As Tom Jones explained:

We are in a tricky business. Many, many financial businesses are businesses where things can easily go wrong if they are not done right. The individual financial control professional must be embedded in the operations. He has to be the number two man. The financial professional in the business has an allegiance to his line business manager but must also wear a corporate hat. He is also my source of information. That is deliberate policy because it builds the financial control function and enables corporate financial control to intervene or mediate in situations where the goals of the individual business unit are in conflict with the overall corporate objective.

But, as noted above, it is not possible to establish the importance of the financial control person by edict in Citicorp's talent-based culture. Credibility is established based on one's expertise and contribution to the business, not one's position in the organizational hierarchy. As Loretta Allen explained in talking about the shift from the conformance to the competitive-team orientation:

People are given more and more responsibility. The financial controllers report directly to the business heads. In the past, they were viewed as merely a compilation group that put together numbers. But before you could expand the role, you had to have the right people. What makes the job are the people. So, the corporation started hiring heavier people.

This quote expresses a theme emphasized throughout the Citicorp interviews—the person-centered professionalism of the financial control function at Citicorp. The financial control philosophy reflects a shared vision of what is expected from a financial professional. Financial control at Citicorp is implemented through people not through an elaborate set of rules and regulations. Loretta Allen talked about what Tom Jones expects from a financial professional:

People are placed in the key areas and are expected to become part of their business units. They have to get the respect of their line managers before their roles expand. There is a vision of what the financial person should be, but you have to get the right person for the job.

Ken Wormser, Financial Controller of the Global Finance Business that includes commercial and investment banking operations in North America, articulated the person-centered philosophy of the financial control organization in the following way:

The history of financial control is based on the people who are running the organization, people in their jobs, and your credibility in the organization. A financial job can be a numbers job or it can be part of the business. The effectiveness of the financial function depends on the people you have in the jobs. The group or division executive must have confidence in his financial person—not just a numbers cruncher, but someone who can help him think through his business. The financial person must have a value-added perspective—know the business, have business judgment.

By defining professionalism in terms of technical competence and individual responsibility, Citicorp reinforces the decentralization philosophy by building control into the fabric of decision making within each business unit. By being integral members of the business teams, the financial professionals develop the necessary intimate understanding of the business needed to maintain control throughout the organization. They understand financial risk and financial discipline. In a firm experiencing rapid change stemming from financial deregulation and business diversification, this balance of financial risk and financial discipline is critical to success. Tom Jones explained:

> The business units are responsible for the integrity of the numbers. Getting better people, professional people, changing the type of people to professional people has allowed the decentralization of financial responsibility.

The financial professionals are given a great deal of discretion in how they manage the risk/discipline tension. In the following quote, Roger Trupin, recently named Controller of Citicorp, and Marjorie Marker, head of the Accounting Policy & Advisory Group, emphasized the opportunity for individuals to have a significant impact on Citicorp:

> The culture is to let people have plenty of responsibility. People at Citicorp are not afraid to do something new. It is almost expected. The culture was brought in by Wriston. People like the ability to be responsible for making very significant decisions.

Echoing the competitive spirit of the overall corporate culture, Loretta Allen described the business-focused, competitive nature of the control function in the following way:

> There is a natural competitiveness between the financial people and the business people, as well as competitiveness between the group financial people and the corporate financial people. This natural tension provides checks and balances within the system.

Within this highly charged, competitive-team culture at Citicorp, the financial professional simultaneously supports and disciplines the decision-making process. Dual responsibility means servicing internal clients while preserving the integrity of the financial reporting system. A professional's ability to say no to a business manager and maintain the business manager's respect and confidence is largely a function of the financial controller's credibility in supporting the internal client in the past. Loretta Allen spoke of the challenge faced in walking this tightrope:

> You have to have a bunch of strong-spirited, aggressive people who are control-oriented, who can rein in business managers without dampening their spirits. Now that is the control challenge. How you do that is by getting the right people in the financial control positions. You have to be able to go head to head with the business people. You have to say, Wait a minute. This is a very nice idea, but its got holes in it.

Sean Rogan, Sector Controller, echoed Tom Jones' comments about the functional responsibility to insure the integrity of the financial system:

> A financial controller has a business and a corporate function. He is the conscience of the corporation in the individual businesses. He has to maintain the integrity of the financials and yet, at the same time, provide a service to the entrepreneurs and businessmen.

Thus we see in Citicorp a reaffirmation of the inevitable tension between independence and involvement faced by the financial professional. It never goes away; it is only managed more or less successfully.

Managing the Financial Function

In keeping with the decentralized character of Citicorp, Tom Jones does not control the resources business units devote to financial control. Each division decides what it will spend on financial control. As long as the control person is the number two person in the business unit, and the single-stream reporting system is being maintained and functioning properly, Jones does not intervene. This philosophy stands in stark contrast to 3M's philosophy. At 3M, a firm of equal diversification and entrepreneurial spirit, the CFO exerts strong head count control over the financial staffing in the various product organizations. At Citicorp, the financial executives were both explicit and emphatic about the control philosophy. As Tom Jones explained:

> Corporate financial control does not monitor or set a limit on the costs for the financial function at the business unit level. We trust their [the divisions'] judge-

ment. It is not our responsibility to know how many heads the businesses have involved in financial control or to mandate a minimum or maximum number.

Tom Jones' philosophy is to concentrate on the quality, rather than the quantity, of the resources going into financial control. The first and foremost means of implementing this philosophy is through the financial professional. Quality is monitored in three ways.

First, the corporate group plays a strong role in recruiting and maintains a career-tracking system to insure career development. Citicorp originally went outside the industry to hire the key people to start the financial control function but now brings both outside and inside professionals into the control function. Citicorp recruits individuals with "an accounting, CPA-technical background" and "MBAs from the analysis side." Citicorp then attempts to integrate the two types of individuals to obtain the balance necessary to develop professionals who can function as integral members of their respective business teams. As Tom Jones explained:

> Effective financial control requires strong accounting and analysis skills. Financial control at the business unit and corporate levels needs the talents of both CPAs and MBAs in order to have the appropriate mix of skills.

The net result of the strong emphasis on recruiting and development is that financial control has greater legitimacy within Citicorp, and offers a career path that did not exist in the past. As one staff member put it:

> Before Jones, financial control was an experience that someone had to have. But, if you stayed too long, you were considered to be a bean counter. With Jones, that clearly changed. You can now have a rewarding career in financial control.

Second, the vision of the financial professional is accompanied by a set of standards that is used in the peer evaluations of the financial-control systems within the individual business units. There is a sense that as long as the professional standards set at the corporate level are maintained, the qualities of the individual will have a strong influence on how financial control is played out in each business unit. Field operations are monitored in terms of professional standards. At the most basic level, failure to pass an internal audit review demonstrates an individual's inability to meet standards. In addition to the audit reviews, peer financial-control reviews and career-tracking reviews require adherence to a high level of professional standards.

Third, Citicorp has made an extensive commitment to comprehensive individual training. Because of the dynamic and changing nature of the business environment, most of the training that is needed is not available from the outside. The corporate financial control group has had to develop very sophisticated training material from scratch. Anyone at all familiar with the changing nature of global financial markets can appreciate the need for comprehensive training throughout Citicorp or any other financial institution. In the next section, we will focus on how "financial engineering" fits within the vision of a financial professional.

The Accounting Policy & Advisory Group

The increased sophistication, the more integral involvement in business strategy and the commitment to training and development that characterizes Citicorp is possibly best exemplified by the Accounting Policy & Advisory Group. The Accounting Policy & Advisory Group is a corporate unit that provides advice and support to financial product development teams. Many of Citicorp's new financial products are generated by off-balance sheet financing needs and revenue recognition issues. It is a fact of life that accounting rules often dictate the viability and profitability of these financial products to the bank. The inevitable result of this set of circumstances is that accounting expertise is an essential part of new financial product development. The required expertise resides in the Accounting Policy & Advisory Group.

Financial Engineering

Since deregulation, Citicorp's business environment has been changing at a pace that is similar to what AT&T is just beginning to experience. The term "financial engineering," which did not exist prior to deregulation, is now a succinct way of describing how the Accounting Policy & Advisory Group adds value to Citicorp and makes the financial control professionals integral members of the business unit teams. According to Marjorie Marker, head of Accounting Policy:

> We consider our group to be financial engineers. It really is what we do. We help
> engineer financial transactions. Accounting is an integral part of a financial trans-
> action and therefore we have to be a part of the product team in order to make

the product viable. The business people need us to manufacture the product. The accounting is crucial to new products and when you want to innovate. They come to us asking for help. If the transactions have adverse accounting "side effects," clients won't do them even if the transactions make economic sense.

The business people know how to structure for the market. They need to know if they can achieve their financial accounting goals.

We will work with them to find a structure that is defensible and will meet their objectives. If there is a conflict between their ultimate goal and the financial accounting objective, we will help them restructure it if it can be done—get the product they want, at the right price, and with the right accounting.

However, you have to remember that while our businesses are noted for pushing the development on creative financial engineering, we, on the accounting side have to be comfortable that any accounting advice we give is prudent and could withstand external scrutiny. The bottom line is, "Would we be comfortable explaining our rationale to the SEC?"

At Citicorp, in contrast to the five industrial firms in the study, accounting is more than a straightforward means for measuring and reporting transactions that have already occurred. Accounting expertise represents a distinct competitive advantage because of the role it plays in the development of new financial product offerings. In the following comment, Marjorie Marker emphasized the strong service and team orientation of the Accounting Policy Group. True to the notion of a financial professional, Accounting Policy Group staff members are expected to develop an internal clientele based on the quality of services they provide and the professional reputation that they build;

The accounting policy people are evaluated by the following they develop. They have to be responsive and give good service. Are they giving good and timely advice? Do they add value? They are very, very service-oriented. They are integral members of the team that constructs the transaction. They have to add value or go elsewhere.

Ms. Marker sees herself as a member of the project teams and has plenty of "tombstones" in her office. (These "tombstones" are awarded to each member of the team as evidence of closing successful transactions.)

Accounting Risk

The emphasis on financial engineering at Citicorp cannot be divorced from a discussion of "accounting risk." The new Financial Risk Advisory Group (which is a spin off of the Accounting Policy Group) represents a formal dedication of corporate resources that is intended to enhance the role of the financial controller in risk management, including the accounting risk. Just what is "accounting risk?" According to Loretta Allen, the head of this group:

> The first part of the accounting risk consideration is that our results may be misleading. It is information risk that may affect decision making. For example, inappropriately taking the profit up front on a financial transaction and not leaving anything to cover the risks in the next three years, well, that's wrong. It is misleading for management as well as external purposes.

> When I'm talking about accounting risk, I'm talking about the risk of measuring something inappropriately and hence distorting management's assessment of the risks and rewards of a particular product or job.

> The second consideration has to do with following an accounting practice that is so inappropriate that the SEC, the regulators, or other external party comes in and criticizes our accounting in the marketplace so that we lose credibility. A loss of credibility can be particularly devastating to a financial institution that must seek funds from the public.

> As a cutting-edge company, as Citicorp, when we do a deal everybody goes through it with a fine-tooth comb and that means it better be clean because someone's going to find the flaw if there is one.

The emphasis in Loretta Allen's comments seems not to be so much on serving the team (although that is clearly a function of Allen's group), as much as in insuring accountability and balanced risk taking. In this case, the disciplining function seems more prominent than the service function. This came through in the following comments by Ms. Allen:

> For example, investment bankers operate in competitive and complicated markets where they have to be aggressive in order to survive. The financial controller has to gain the respect of these high-powered businessmen to insure that the profits are appropriately recognized, particularly when that recognition will span several years. Our goal is to give the financial controllers technical competence and personal confidence so they can succeed in their jobs.

Yet, this characterization oversimplifies the interaction between the Financial Risk Advisory Group and the product people. Loretta Allen uses the language of risk and return to define a shared objective and responsibility. Just as the product people manage and take responsibility for business risk, the financial organization manages and takes responsibility for the accounting risk and becomes an integral participant in risk management.

Relationship to the FASB

The Accounting Policy & Advisory Group, as well as Financial Risk Advisory, also plays a role in interacting with and influencing the promulgations of the Financial Accounting Standards Board. Financial services firms, such as Citicorp, share a particularly strong interest in the deliberations of the FASB. Because the viability and profitability of many of its financial products are tied to accounting rules governing off-balance sheet transactions and profit recognition issues on financial instruments and transactions, the pronouncements of the FASB can have a direct and substantial effect on Citicorp's bottom line.

Citicorp has three concerns when it comes to the FASB: 1) the FASB's direct impact on Citicorp's bottom line, 2) the costs of complying with FASB regulations, and 3) the need to make the FASB more accountable for its actions. Roger Trupin, Marjorie Marker, and Loretta Allen all expressed concern about the impact of the FASB. As Marjorie Marker explained:

> Where there are no set accounting rules, financial accounting risk comes from the potential for being second guessed when the FASB finally looks at a new transaction/product. Unfavorable accounting for either the bank or the client can virtually destroy an economically justified product. We have to be actively involved in the standard-setting process in order to have a sense of where the FASB will come out on these cutting-edge accounting issues, to educate them as to the substance of these new financial products and finally to convey to the FASB our views of the appropriate accounting so that a reasonable accounting rule results.

> Being on FASB Task Forces, industry committees, and AICPA technical committees provides us with this accounting "intelligence" that we believe gives us a competitive edge. We've followed this active course for a long time, and many companies are now seeing the business benefits of being active in the accounting area.

The job of the Accounting Policy Group is to develop this market intelligence, and, even more significantly, to influence FASB's deliberations. The following quotes indicate that Citicorp takes this function quite seriously. With respect to the costs of regulation, which leads directly into the issue of greater accountability for the board, Roger Trupin was particularly frank:

> The FASB is coming out with too much and requiring business to change too often. It is becoming very expensive, adding so much cost base to U.S. industry, especially when we are trying to be competitive. It has gotten out of hand, and the rules and opinions that they are coming out with are so complex that I imagine that college professors are even having trouble understanding them . . . Get some of your students to evaluate the usefulness of a cash flow statement for a financial institution. There's a lot of data in that statement but very little useful information.

> The banking community's voice is heard a lot more and we think we are making some progress. The Groves task force [Ray Groves, managing partner for Ernst and Whinney] just issued its report. Through John Reed's activities on the Business Roundtable's Accounting Principles Task Force, we have challenged the Financial Accounting Foundation and the FASB to improve the standard-setting process.

These last comments establish the fact that members of the financial organization are participating in the business on all fronts. The Accounting Policy & Advisory Group exemplifies the change from being bookkeepers and bean counters to being valued financial professionals.

Case Summary and the Conceptual Model

Using our conceptual model, the foregoing analysis has documented the dramatic shift that Citicorp's financial organization has undergone over the past decade. We believe that the analysis provides convincing evidence of the existence of a distinct financial-function orientation, of the types of factors that determine this orientation, and of the impact this orientation has on the configuration of financial work within Citicorp.

Citicorp has made a transition from a strong conformance to an equally strong competitive-team orientation. This shift in orientation has been driven by 1) significant increases in competitiveness, complexity, and risk stemming from changes in business environment and business strategy, and 2) the commitment of Walter Wriston and John Reed to build a quality financial control function at the corporate and business levels. The earlier conformance orientation was driven by the highly stable and regulated nature of the financial services industry prior to the 1970s. The control organization was relegated to largely technical functions. Current conditions of deregulation and diversification, on the other hand, demand a larger and more sophisticated financial control function.

The competitive-team orientation has clearly been influenced by the extremely decentralized, highly entrepreneurial, person-centered Citicorp culture. The character of the competitive-team orientation is also influenced by the character of the financial services industry. The seamless computer-based operating and financial controls, as well as the central importance of accounting in the engineering of new financial products, provide natural linkages for integrating financial expertise and control into business strategy, product development and operations.

The speed with which Citicorp has made the transition from the conformance to the competitive-team orientation is due in part to the decision made early on by Walter Wriston to hire individuals from outside the firm for assistance in establishing an innovative financial control function.

The overwhelming theme that emerges from the Citicorp interviews is the absolute requirement for a financial control staff that is "close to the business." The most significant preconditions for sound financial control lie in having a group of financial professionals who understand the business and are included in the formulation and management of business plans and operations. Control is best established by providing a service that is valued by business managers and product people.

4

3M

The story of 3M's financial function describes an organization that is responding to significant changes in business strategy while keeping a lid on the amount of resources devoted to financial control. In large part, due to the history of financial control within 3M, the senior financial management group faces two significant challenges: 1) the challenge of being involved with the business units while maintaining an independent corporate perspective, and 2) the challenge of supporting the business unit customers while continuing to reduce the costs of providing financial services through the use of the latest computer technology. 3M is a prime example of a firm trying to "do more with less."

While the 3M story does not entail the dramatic shift in orientation precipitated by competitive crisis or radical deregulation as in the Ford, Citicorp, and AT&T cases, 3M's story does provide insight into the challenge of managing the financial function in a firm widely admired and extolled for its innovative excellence. Based upon 3M's ranking as one of America's top five most-admired corporations in the 1989 and 1990 *Fortune Magazine* survey, 3M appears to be an organization that successfully combines a competitive-team orientation at the business level with a command-and-control orientation at the corporate level. As the interview comments suggest, the financial organization is expected to balance the dual responsibilities of being involved with the business units while maintaining an independent corporate perspective.

Roger Roberts, Senior Vice President, Finance, pointed out that the current financial organization has evolved in response to management decisions made in the 1940s and 1950s:

> First, a little history on the company. Back in the 1940s and 1950s, the company took a strong position towards the value of research and development, and subsequent new product flow, keeping close to the customer and his needs, plus

developing a very efficient, high quality, manufacturing and distribution process. The early management of the company, in their wisdom, decided the best organizational structure to accomplish this was to keep the business units rather small and focused on fairly narrow industry segments. They also felt that the resources within the company—be they technical, marketing, or manufacturing—would be available to all businesses to best serve the needs of their specific customers in a very cost-effective manner.

The result of this is that through the years the company developed into an ever-growing array of new businesses involving a variety of industries and geographical locations. Also demonstrated during those years was the fact that these business had to operate in a very flexible and in an ever-changing environment. In other words, the businesses were always going through phases of restructuring, dividing and growing, and the like.

Implied in this, is an environment that is rather undisciplined and allows the various business units much freedom in developing their own marketing approaches, research approaches, manufacturing and distribution. Also implied in this is that a large degree of resource sharing would take place within the company. It's out of this culture and environment that 3M's basic accounting and financial control system evolved.

Basically, the new accounting system had to do a number of things:

1) Be able to accomplish a meaningful allocation in the recharging of these resources to the various business units.

2) Provide corporate management with a financial reporting system that gave them a valid and comparable reading of the financial results of the various units.

3) Provide for the ever-changing restructuring of the businesses.

4) Provide for a consistent and strong discipline in financial matters within the management of the business units.

The fundamental management operating philosophy at 3M (which has not changed for approximately 50 years) is to allow the business units freedom to operate in undisciplined environments. The corporate financial organization has the responsibility to provide financial discipline primarily through the accounting system. Of all the executives included in the study, 3M financial executives discuss matters of financial control primarily from a systems perspective. Roger Roberts indicated that in order to develop its basic control system (the commodity P&L system), 3M felt it needed to have a "strong financial and accounting organization. This is essentially the organization we have today."

In terms of our conceptual model, we believe that 3M's financial function falls somewhere between the command-and-control and competitive-team orientations. When not talking specifically about the commodity P&L system, interviewees at 3M are as likely to talk about independence, administrative efficiency, corporate ownership, and their stewardship responsibilities (characteristic of a command-and-control orientation), as they are likely to talk about providing leadership in the financial area, being involved with the business units and providing sophisticated analysis (characteristic of a competitive-team orientation).

We begin the 3M story with a discussion of the changes that 3M's business organization is currently undergoing. As a corporate staff function, it is the responsibility of the financial organization to make whatever changes are necessary to support the business units while maintaining an independent, corporate perspective.

Systems Performance and Professional Sophistication

3M's current corporate strategy includes implementing a global product organization and, in this country, substantially increasing its government business. In combination, these two strategic initiatives are having a significant impact on the financial organization. The move to a global product organization required the financial organization to modify the accounting system to produce contribution margin financial statements on a global basis. This systems challenge has been accomplished. The senior financial managers at 3M are now focusing their attention on upgrading the sophistication of the financial professionals who are assigned to the business units.

When 3M decided to enlarge the scope of its research and development business with the government, the financial organization had to superimpose a government accounting financial system over its basic accounting system. According to Roger Roberts, the government accounting challenge has been pretty much resolved from a systems perspective. On the cost side, 3M estimates that doing contract research and development business with the government will require six to eight times more financial controls than are required on the commercial side of the business. The financial controls are estimated to be a fairly significant part of the total contract price.

When it comes to the systems side of the financial organization, all management needs have been incorporated into the accounting system. The unresolved pressures really apply to "the people side" of the financial organization. Within the 3M culture, there are strong corporate pressures to keep a lid on the growth of administrative costs. Given 3M's strong commitment to head count control in the corporate staff areas, the financial organization is trying to accommodate the business strategy-related staffing increases without increasing the total investment in the financial organization.

3M is trying to meet the needs of the business units through efficiencies gained by the use of computer technology in the transaction processing areas. 3M is trying to become more efficient while simultaneously trying to increase the sophistication of its business unit controllers. Changes in 3M's international operations are indicative of the challenges facing the financial organization. These changes are described in the following paragraphs.

International Operations

The move to integrate international operations into a global product organization is part of 3M's efforts to be a more effective global competitor. According to Jim Schoenwetter, 3M's Corporate Controller:

> The product, versus geography, is the direction 3M is moving in. There is still an international VP but the international staff group has been disbanded and integrated back into the line and staff units. Each division has an international person.

> You have the sector that allocates the resources, the group that defines the strategy, and the division that implements it. If you are going to implement on a global basis, you need input. In the past there was greater separation between the U.S. and the international operations. We can no longer stand the separation and need to integrate. A division controller never went out of the U.S. A division GM had little or no responsibility outside the U.S.

Jim Schoenwetter made the following remark in commenting on the greater sophistication required of divisional controllers:

> What is different is that we are now implementing on a global basis and that implementation takes you down to the division GM level. It is a new challenge for the division controllers [50 division controllers]. Most significant implication—what does 3M expect from them?

As financial leaders to the business units, which is what we articulate and the business people want, you then, as my business leader, must be able to at least keep me out of trouble tax-wise, know the role of internal auditing, help with receivables, tell me if I am going to have a problem accruing for pollution control costs and offer more help on a wider variety of issues.

In essence, Jim Schoenwetter is arguing that the complexity of the global business environment has created a need for a divisional CFO. The tradition at 3M has been that the divisional controllers progress up the ranks from cost or management accountants to become controllers. This tradition is currently being reexamined.

Divisional controllers must now have broader knowledge of a number of different technical skills and must extend themselves beyond a cost accounting mentality. The controllers must have a more intimate knowledge of their business if they are to serve as the chief financial advisors to their divisional general managers. It is within the context of the divisional CFO that 3M's financial executives stressed the need to develop the leadership abilities of the business controllers.

If the divisional controllers are going to be financial leaders within their business units, they must 1) develop their communication and interpersonal skills, 2) become more proactive in the management of the business units, and 3) become better people managers.

Financial Leaders Within the Business Units

Buck Menssen, Staff Vice President of Tax Operations and former sector controller, was quite outspoken on the need to develop interpersonal skills:

Twenty-five years ago most of the people [in the financial organization] were not accountants. The controller had a music degree. These people had excellent communication and persuasion skills. They did not have good analytical skills. That was our problem at the time. 3M then swung to the analytic skills.

Buck Menssen, in a group interview with the current CFO, Roger Roberts, and the Treasurer, Ralph Ebbott, expressed the group's concern that the financial organization has become too technocratic, leading to a leadership vacuum:

Finance people are the ones who should at least keep the economic perspective of what we are doing and should not allow people to do things from either a social or political position that does not make sense economically . . . And I think the finance community has lost the handle on it. I think one of the reasons we have lost the handle on it is that we have become technocrats in analytical work. We have become good analysts and we know what to do. But I think our interpersonal skills, persuasion skills have dropped.

There is a strong feeling by the senior controllers in the controller's group [sector controllers] that we have now switched to a lot of analytical people who never leave their desks, who have zero power and persuasion over anybody.

Analytical skills are necessary but insufficient qualifications for the divisional CFO of the future. Financial control at 3M is going beyond analysis to include leadership and decision-making skills. Buck Menssen continued:

Quality here at 3M in the finance area is more than having an analytical statement that is correct. Quality also includes selling it and getting it processeu through and understood by management and acted upon . . . Quality takes it all the way through the service as we do in selling. It is just not selling the product, not just making the product. It is the whole process of servicing the customer is where quality is. We have got to understand that more in finance. Producing an accurate P&L statement is not sufficient quality. You have got to sell it . . .

In addition to leadership, 3M executives stressed the importance of people management. Jim Schoenwetter was very explicit on this matter. In discussing the factors most critical to the success of a controller, he cited credibility, respect by management, insight and vision, outside recognition and people management skills:

You have to demonstrate that you can lead people. Other people, sector heads, will not listen to you . . . if you have inept people on your staff.

In the future, we need people who are good accountants, service the business units, and will be able to manage people and lead their own staffs. You can be a professional advisor and be very effective at the business level. You can be a damn good accountant and have people as mad as wet hens and as unmotivated as can be working for you.

Taken together, the comments made by Jim Schoenwetter and Buck Menssen indicate that 3M has emphasized impersonal analysis and being "good accountants" over the last twenty-five years or so, with less attention being paid to the communicative and interpersonal side of the financial organization. This emphasis on impersonal analysis can only be understood within the context of the tradition of centralized financial control at 3M.

The Tradition of Centralized Financial Control at 3M

The emphasis throughout the interviews on developing leadership capabilities and communication skills, and becoming more people-oriented indicates that 3M's financial executives see people development as the route to take in supporting the competitive-team orientation of the business units. However, any efforts to increase the sophistication of the financial staff (primarily business unit controllers) must be consistent with 3M's long-standing philosophies of independent, centralized, financial control and strong head-count control over corporate staff functions.

The challenges that the senior financial management group faces cannot be understood without some additional knowledge of the history and tradition of financial control at 3M. This history and tradition date back to the first CEO, William McKnight, who started out as a bookkeeper. Of all the firms in the study, 3M is possibly the best example of a living history and culture that literally goes back to the founding fathers of the firm. McKnight established the well-known "grow and divide" intrapreneurial philosophy of 3M, as popularized by Peters and Waterman in their bestseller *In Search of Excellence*. What is less well known about McKnight's legacy is his attempt to balance a strong decentralized, market-based, business organization with a highly centralized structure of corporate staff units, including engineering, personnel and finance.

In explaining McKnight's influence on 3M's financial organization, Roger Roberts, Senior Vice President, Finance, elaborates on 3M's brand of matrix organization that is described in the opening paragraphs of the 3M story:

> McKnight and subsequent CEOs were strong on keeping the business units small and focused as we grew, because that was the easiest way of making sure we had good contacts with industry. It would not dissolve because it is now part of a big company. As soon as something got pretty good size, divide it up. The basic culture is to divide up things, make things small to grow fast.

Corporate management foresaw that, OK, we are going to have out in the future a lot of these little business units running around. We have got to have some common threads here to make sure that they do not get too wild, off the beaten path from what we want the corporation doing. We have got to have a strong, centralized, financial control system . . . The culture plays a big part in how the financial function is organized.

3M's financial organization is centralized both in terms of reporting relationships and the physical location of the financial staff in St. Paul, Minnesota and now in Austin, Texas. All financial staff are assigned to the business units and report up through the financial organization to the CFO. The level of financial staffing for the divisions is budgeted and controlled by the financial organization. All inventory and cost accounting tasks are performed at corporate headquarters. 3M's financial organization, therefore, maintains a very high degree of locational centralization to go along with its organizational centralization.

Another aspect of the tradition of centralized financial control is the emphasis placed on productivity improvement and head-count control. Since staff functions such as finance and personnel do not report through the business units, there is no "bottom line" control over the size of these functions. 3M believes that without bottom line control (which is not part of the current management philosophy), centralized staff functions have a tendency to expand at the expense of the business operations. To counter this tendency, there is a strong emphasis on head count control, and on meeting new staffing requirements out of productivity improvements achieved elsewhere within each function. As Ted Stromberg, Assistant Controller for Accounting Systems, explained:

We must be concerned about structure in major corporations. The structure can bury you. And the structure can just grow because people want to know more and more . . . As a staff organization, our effectiveness and spending has to be really watched. It is an area that can grow very quickly without the controls a business unit could put on.

Roger Roberts indicated that the emphasis on head-count control extends beyond the staff organizations:

We are under certain corporate philosophies and one of the philosophies is [that] you should have continuous improvement in productivity in your organization. This is corporate-wide. You should always have a continuing emphasis on the productivity of corporate management.

This head-count control philosophy has received increased emphasis under the current cost-reduction program initiated in the mid '80s. Since the financial organization is the corporate staff group most closely identified with cost control, it has been under a certain amount of pressure to lead by example in reducing head count.

Thus, in spite of the much publicized corporate philosophy of decentralized business unit management, 3M maintains a philosophy of highly centralized financial control. 3M's financial executives talk competitive-team but operate under a corporate philosophy of command and control. Efficient use of corporate resources, continuous improvement in corporate staff functions and corporate staff head-count control fit the command-and-control orientation extremely well.

Between Competitive-Team and Command-and-Control: Managing the Challenge of Involvement and Independence

Traditional management operating philosophies, such as 3M's, establish a check and balance culture of involvement and independence. Even when it is involved in the business, a separate financial organization is also charged with the responsibility of making objective, independent assessments on behalf of the corporation. The financial management challenge is to maintain a balance between being involved and independent.

In interviews conducted for an article that appeared in the February, 1986 issue of *Management Accounting*, 3M's financial executives described their operating philosophy in terms quite in keeping with the competitive-team orientation. Harry A. Hammerly, CFO at the time, enunciated the principles of involvement, partnership, and credibility based on expertise in the following manner:

> I tell our people, "Eliminate the word devil's advocate from your vocabulary. Your job is to help the operating people achieve what they're trying to achieve. Then if you have to say no, you'll be respected for it." The first priority is working with operating people. (Williams, 1986, p. 4)

This need to be involved in the businesses was reiterated and reinforced throughout that article. In our interviews, Jim Schoenwetter talked of the controller's customer-service orientation:

> Quality of service [meeting customer expectations] is one of the pegs which is allowing us to change. We are putting a great deal of emphasis on defining what our customer wants and then periodically measuring against that. If we were a stand-alone business unit, we would get hired and paid, or not hired and starve.

> Our customers [both internal and external] . . . We have to keep them happy. We have to work with internal [staff] functions, but really the line units [are our main customer].

Clearly, the language of teamwork, of service to and involvement with the line operations, exists at 3M. However, movement toward greater service and involvement has to be consistent with independence and centralization. The role of the finance organization in corporate oversight as an independent, third-party observer of business operations cannot be ignored. As interviewed for the *Management Accounting* article, Roger Roberts, then Corporate Controller, put it this way:

> 3M's management wants a good, objective financial reading as to what's really going on. Therefore, we have a controllers' group to serve in that capacity. That's one of our biggest functions—to provide a very independent, objective viewpoint of the financial performance of the business. (Williams, 1986, p. 2)

The independent analyst role was also voiced in the interviews conducted in this study. But beyond independence, there is also oversight. Two different financial executives made the following comments:

> The history of 3M that goes back to Bill McKnight is that finance is a strong arm of the corporation. They are part of the team that makes us succeed.

> Jacobson and Hammerly both reaffirmed the need for a strong independent function. Line people can get in trouble in a hurry without proper guidance or financial objectives. There is a history of credibility going way back to early relationships. No one is a stranger to anyone else.

At 3M, a competitive-team orientation has to coexist with a command-and-control orientation.

Within the context of this study, the single most important resource in centralized financial control, as pointed out by all the senior financial executives, is 3M's commodity P&L system. The commodity P&L system is the backbone of centralized financial control at 3M.

The Commodity P&L System: The Backbone of the Financial Organization

Like Merck and Citicorp, 3M has an integrated system of financial and management accounting information that feeds into a single financial performance evaluation system. 3M calls it its commodity P&L system. The commodity P&L system is something that 3M takes for granted. However, from our research perspective, the commodity P&L system is a strategic asset of the financial organization. The commodity P&L system provides highly efficient and uniform management reporting across 3M's 50 or so product divisions. But more important, the commodity P&L system is an indispensable tool in the strategic management of the firm. The system permits corporate, sector, division, and business unit managers to monitor the profitability of some 3,500 product groupings (commodities). According to Roger Roberts:

> We do not have a fixed organization. The financial system has to have a lot of flexibility. There is one common building block—commodities—that we think will be moved around. There are 3,000 plus commodities with full P&Ls. We can go sector, group, division, to commodity. We have a history of continually reorganizing. Ted, Ted Stromberg, Assistant Controller for Systems, just moves the blocks over to the new organization. Over a five-year period, here is what we are going to sell, the cost structure, the investment.

Ted Stromberg elaborated on the fundamentals of the commodity P&L system:

> 3M allocates all costs back to its divisions. All costs go back for performance evaluation. That is what it costs to run the business. The divisions can argue over the costs. 3M allocates assets on a quarterly basis. 3M puts out over 3,000 P&L statements monthly and ROCE [return on capital employed] statements quarterly.
>
> Operational issues drive data needs. We are driven by markets and technology. Operating businesses are driven by their markets. There is a direct link from markets and technology to the commodity P&L system.
>
> 3M's Board just created two new operating groups. The thirteen digit code in the accounting system allows the financial organization to meet the data needs of top management quite easily.

The commodity P&L system represents the backbone of 3M's finance organization and the entire firm. 3M managers have relied on the system for much of the company's history. The commodity P&L system is tangible evidence that a centralized financial control organization can contribute to a decentralized business organization. Ted Stromberg traced the history of the commodity P&L system back to the early '30s and linked the system to the management philosophy of "grow and divide." Since that time, 3M has incorporated the latest technology into producing the 3,500 commodity P&Ls.

The commodity P&L system is suggestive of the strong historical contribution that the financial organization has made to 3M's success. But there are new challenges facing the financial organization. One challenge of particular significance comes right from the CEO. The current CEO, Allen Jacobson, has reinforced the use of financial targets in strategic planning and business performance evaluation. Jacobson has created a demand for financial information throughout 3M that might not have been as strong if the CEO was not as numbers oriented. Roger Roberts commented on the CEO's expectations from the financial organization:

> The CEO wants to be aware of what is going on in all aspects of finance. Keep 3M out of trouble in future years. Start restructuring today to fit the future. Be proactive with the business units. Keep focused on the financial results. He wants us to continue to develop a keen awareness amongst all our management people on financial concerns so that they are financially literate. There is an educative role, always. One half of our job from a management standpoint in finance is educating people.

Financial Measures

The current CEO, Allen Jacobson, has reinforced the importance of financial targets in strategy formulation and business performance evaluation. Both Jacobson and the previous CFO, Harry Hammerly, advocated the move back to return on capital employed (ROCE) as the key measure of financial performance rather than sales growth. Jacobson and Hammerly just reinforced the long-standing (but temporarily forgotten) emphasis on financial performance measurement. Roger Roberts explained:

> The philosophy goes back to McKnight. This company is going to be 1) a growth company, 2) a company that finances growth from earnings, 3) a company that pays out a fair dividend to shareholders, and to accomplish that, you need, 4) a ROCE of 27 percent or better. We have never had a high debt/equity ratio.

He [previous controller Harry Hammerly] helped clarify the corporate objectives. The objectives changed from sales growth to growth in earnings. We all know there is a [sales] growth objective but it is not stated in sales terms. Now [it is] EPS growth.

3M now has an earnings growth goal, ROCE, ROE, new products. We measure this. We used to have sales growth and profit margin targets, but the emphasis changed to assets. Must grow and get the returns. This change in emphasis in 1982 was a good change.

The explicit emphasis on financial measures in performance evaluation has created a demand for financial services over and above the demand created by the government business and international product organization strategies. Although financial targets have always been important to 3M's success, the shift to (or back to) EPS growth, ROCE, and ROE around 1982 seems to be a significant event affecting the financial organization.

Case Summary and the Conceptual Model

With respect to our conceptual model, 3M's financial organization would fall somewhere between command-and-control and competitive-team. 3M's senior financial management group talks about a competitive-team orientation within a corporate operating philosophy of command-and-control.

Since 3M has a history of incorporating change into the capabilities of its financial and accounting systems as a matter of course, the drama of crisis cannot be used to make the 3M story more titillating. But the 3M story is a good story. Rather than trying to force 3M into someone else's mold, we will use an extended quote from Roger Roberts to summarize the 3M story:

...this environment of change in recent years has put pressures on our finance organization in terms of an ever-increasing rate of providing more services with relatively stable budget constraints. This has meant we had to adopt some overall philosophies as to what changes are going to take place in the future within the organization. Our professional people are going to have to be more self-sufficient, more professional, more analytical in their approach to their jobs. They also have to develop a more global perspective to their responsibilities. It also means that the environment they work in has to have a continuing emphasis on productivity improvements, improved quality in our services, and innovation.

The end result of all this is that our workload has to change from one of process-ing and analyzing data to one of providing counseling and analysis to the busi-ness units. It also means that we will continue to have to balance objective reporting on the financial results of the business units with providing for the financial requirements needed by the business units.

This has always been a tough area to balance and one that has always required us in the past—and will require us in the future—to handle this area of conflict. Prioritization is the answer.

The 3M case provides insights into the thinking processes of a man-agement team that has been quite open about the challenges the financial management team faces in a firm widely extolled for its innovative excel-lence. The case documents the challenges involved when strong impera-tives of centralized financial control and administrative efficiency stand alongside a team-oriented business-unit operating philosophy

5
AT&T

The story of the financial organization cannot be separated from AT&T's transition from being a regulated domestic monopoly, to becoming a deregulated global competitor. The transition has had an extraordinary impact on the financial organization. The shift from regulation to competition is mirrored in fundamental changes in the financial organization. AT&T's financial function, which was once described as a complex bookkeeping operation devoted to the technical administration of externally imposed rules and regulations, is now trying to become a professional financial organization emphasizing sophisticated financial analysis and support to the business units. The shift in the role and mission of the financial organization affects the people, the resources, and the structure of the function. Every aspect of AT&T's financial organization is currently undergoing significant change.

To their credit, AT&T's financial executives have recognized that a change in mission is not possible without a change in culture. In terms of our conceptual model, a change in the mission of the financial organization must be grounded in a shift in operating philosophy from a conformance to a competitive-team orientation.

The AT&T story provides the best empirical description of the conformance orientation to financial control. Even though Perry Colwell, Senior Vice President for Financial Management, stresses the strong command-and-control orientation surrounding AT&T's past functional organization, the impact of divestiture and deregulation is a story best told as movement away from conformance to competitive-team. Since Citicorp has already made the shift away from conformance to competitive-team, conformance is more of a memory of a past culture. AT&T is currently in the midst of changing its culture. Some of the management decisions that go along with a change in culture require substantial reductions in the work force and reallocations of personnel out of accounting and finance and into line operations.

If AT&T's financial organization is going to achieve the legitimacy and credibility that Citicorp's financial organization has achieved, it must move away from being perceived as "green-eyeshade accountants" and move toward being considered financial professionals. While AT&T and Citicorp share much in common as regulated enterprises, there are some obvious and very important differences between the two firms. Five differences immediately come to mind. First, the conformance orientation that management must change at AT&T is probably stronger than at Citicorp by virtue of the public service heritage and regulated monopoly character of "Ma Bell." Second, divestiture and deregulation have caused abrupt versus gradual change. Court rulings and regulatory changes require immediate managerial responses. Third, AT&T has undergone a constant wave of internal restructurings as management has searched for the best "market-facing" organizational structure. Fourth, reductions in AT&T's revenue stream (at divestiture) have forced significant reductions in financial staffing levels. And, finally, deeply embedded work practices and mindsets, stemming from AT&T's heritage as a regulated monopoly, are hard to change in the short run.

The challenges that AT&T managers are facing on all fronts require changes in the fundamental orientation to and configuration of financial work. The "new" AT&T cannot exist with the "old" AT&T financial control system. This case describes the challenges the financial organization is encountering in moving from the "green-eyeshade accountant" role to the "financial professional" role. The AT&T case points out most clearly the differences between the conformance and competitive-team orientations, much as the Ford case points out most clearly the differences between the command-and-control and competitive-team orientations.

The Context of Change at AT&T: Divestiture and Deregulation

With divestiture and deregulation, AT&T has experienced a precipitous change in its business environment. The divestiture of AT&T represents the largest corporate breakup in U.S. history. Accordingly, the task of transitioning from a long-standing, regulated monopoly to a quasi-regulated firm subject to the discipline of the market has been called the most significant managerial challenge of the twentieth century The term "culture shock" has been used to convey the magnitude of the change faced by management and employees. AT&T has recognized the need for a total management reorientation from organizationally and functionally separate operations to integrated, market-oriented business units.

For some 70 years, as one of the largest companies in the world, AT&T functioned as a monopoly within a very stable and secure regulated environment. As such, AT&T was assured of the opportunity to generate a steady and reasonable flow of funds through "rate-of-return" regulation. Under rate-of-return regulation, AT&T stockholders were allowed a "fair" rate of return on their investment. Like Citicorp, the greater the asset base, the greater the total dollar return.

The trouble with rate-of-return regulation is that it provides few incentives for cost control. It is more profitable to capitalize costs incurred and "build these costs into the base." As long as management conformed to the wishes of regulators acting in the public interest, AT&T's revenue stream was expected to grow with each approved rate increase. The world of regulation as it existed prior to divestiture did not provide many incentives for reducing costs and rapidly introducing technological innovations. Even though AT&T's pre-divestiture management team, as well as the regulators, were aware of the lack of market incentives for cost control, the functional organization characteristic of a command-and-control orientation was designed to achieve operating efficiencies and promote technological innovations.

However, as a result of two public policy decisions made in the early 1980s, AT&T found itself facing a radically different competitive environment in which success was no longer assured. The competitive environment confronted AT&T with a new set of management challenges for which it was ill-prepared. The two public policy changes were:

1) The FCC decision, effective with the start of 1983, to permit AT&T to compete in the marketplace through the establishment of a separate, unregulated subsidiary; and subsequently,

2) The out-of-court settlement of the Department of Justice antitrust suit against AT&T, that took effect in 1984, in which AT&T agreed to divest itself of its intra-state operating companies. In return, AT&T was given greater freedom to compete in the data processing and telecommunications markets, except for long-distance services. The FCC and state public utility commissions continued to regulate long-distance telephone services.

Under divestiture, the FCC required AT&T to keep its regulated and unregulated businesses physically separated. The FCC was concerned that AT&T might use the returns from its regulated business to cross-subsidize its unregulated businesses. The physical separation requirement proved to be both onerous and inefficient. For example, AT&T was required to maintain two different sales forces even though both sales forces might be serving the same individual or corporate customers. In 1986, the FCC allowed AT&T to physically integrate its regulated and unregulated businesses under the stipulation that AT&T separately account for the regulated and unregulated businesses.

It is true that, upon divestiture, AT&T had more freedom to develop new products and choose new markets in which to compete. However, it would be a gross mistake to characterize AT&T as an unregulated business. Even after divestiture, AT&T's primary business, long-distance telephone services, was still highly regulated, while its competitors, Sprint and MCI, were not regulated. One of the most significant challenges faced by post-divestiture AT&T management has not simply been learning how to compete, but rather how to compete under the handicap of being "the only regulated player in an unregulated market."

In the following comment, Perry Colwell, Senior Vice President for Financial Management, discussed the challenges of dealing with divestiture coupled with continued regulatory constraints:

> As far as for the contingencies the business is facing right now, we are trying to learn how to take a business that was built up over 75 or 100 years and take the piece that remains with us and try to leverage on that business, and be a major player in the information management and movement markets worldwide.

> In doing this, we have a lot of problems, a lot of contingencies . . . One is severe competition . . . In the last eight to ten months in the business market, MCI has been eating our lunch in some of the profitable business markets—WATTS, 800 services—this kind of thing. That's a very big contingency right there . . . If the regulatory environment situation in the United States did not favor MCI and Sprint, AT&T would be a much more effective competitor. So one of things that we are trying to do is get regulatory change . . . to go from rate-of-return regulation to price cap or something [else].

Since the time of the interviews, the FCC has approved "price cap" regulation, which provides AT&T with greater pricing freedom and greater incentives to minimize costs. However, the significance of Perry Colwell's comment is not diminished. AT&T still faces severe competition in its core business.

Megadeals

In addition to facing fierce price competition, AT&T has had to cope with a rapidly changing, and highly complex and risky market. As large corporate and governmental customers seek integrated solutions to their information management needs, suppliers such as AT&T are being forced to compete for "megadeals" consisting of large scale, long-term contracts to provide integrated packages of communication hardware and services.

Roger Davis, recently named Corporate Controller, described the nature of these megadeals and their potential impact on the financial organization:

> As you move into complex offerings to customers . . . possibly to the government or another major company, there's going to be bids put on the table . . . I think one of the things we've seen [is that] the government bidding process for some of these megadeals in the last year or so is probably a precursor of the way this business is going to be over the next twenty-five years.

> . . . Are our internal measurements and management processes up to it? And are we, in the financial team, going to do something stupid that gets in the way of our capability to capitalize on these opportunities or to measure them as they go forward and so forth.

These megadeals require an integrated organizational structure that supports the competitive bidding process and subsequent contract management. The large amount of potential cash flows involved in "megadeal" competition creates a demand for sophisticated financial systems and financial analysis.

AT&T must understand what many interviewees referred to as the "real economics" of these deals. The responsibility for doing the analysis has fallen upon AT&T's financial staff. However, as the preceding comments have indicated, AT&T is handicapped by its history. AT&T has to cope with inadequate financial systems, inexperienced financial staff, and ill-structured measurement and reward systems. Roger Davis talked about the megadeal phenomenon and the leadership his organization must provide:

> Mr. Davis: A lot of these deals as they go down, because they are extremely competitive and inter-departmental in nature, probably on face of it, are not very attractive on the day you bid them. It is going to be made attractive as you work with the customer over time to deploy new technology, and to add value and so forth.

Interviewer: So they're very strategic decisions?

Mr. Davis: Yes . . . I am concerned about how we do our job in the financial community. We must have the proper mechanisms and processes to reinforce a management process that says that we can go in there, we can pay 60 for this company, or can bid this low, and over the next five years we make it right for the AT&T shareholder . . . And, I have got a feeling that if we put in a financial process that is so stringent and structured, we may never win a deal. We may never buy a company.

Without any history of working with the business units to meet competitive challenges, Roger Davis has no basis from which to estimate the impact that changes in the financial organization will have on the business units.

Restructuring to Meet the Imperatives of the Marketplace

Roger Davis has inherited a financial organization that is the amalgamation of at least two separate financial organizations that fit into a highly functional, specialized organizational structure. Prior to divestiture, AT&T was run as separate "product" and "communication services" businesses. Both businesses had relatively predictable markets and profits. The communication business, consisting of the local telephone companies and AT&T long-distance, sold residential and commercial telephone services. The product divisions sold network communication gear to the local and long-distance telephone companies, and telephone equipment to residential customers and businesses. For much of its history, AT&T had been the only player in both these markets. Managing the interdepencies between these businesses was more of a technical matter than a commercial matter. After divestiture, however, the management of these interdependencies has taken on strategic significance.

Prior to divestiture, few incentives existed to promote efficiencies between the two businesses. In fact, AT&T's monopoly status, coupled with rate-of-return regulation, provided few incentives to become efficient. As long as AT&T could justify its cost base, it was guaranteed a "fair" rate of return. As a result, the larger the cost base, the larger the dollar return. Given the lack of any competitive benchmarks, regulators had no basis for challenging the efficiency of AT&T's operations. The net result of this regulatory dynamic is that AT&T evolved into a highly bureaucratic organization characterized by highly functional and redundant product and administrative structures. The interaction between the two "businesses" was an artifact of regulatory demands and bureaucratic growth, not market conditions. However, as noted earlier, the pre-divestiture management team was aware of the inherent shortcomings of the regulated environment. Inefficiencies resulting from a conformance orientation were counteracted through a functional organization oriented to achieving operating efficiencies.

With divestiture and deregulation, AT&T has been forced to confront its now inappropriate, top heavy bureaucracy. One of the most significant challenges still facing AT&T is figuring out how to manage a quasi-regulated business in a competitive market environment. A functional bureaucracy would seem to have to give way, but not all the way, to a highly decentralized yet integrated entrepreneurial structure. As Perry Colwell explained:

> One of the most difficult management challenges we have is how to manage the traditional communication business that has one huge multi-billion dollar network which is a single resource and how to manage that in reasonable parts, business units, SBU's or whatever you want to call them. And to couple the management of that communications business with other non-regulated, product kinds of businesses [PBX's, computers]. We've had a difficult time finding a management structure that will be effective. We're getting closer . . . For a long time, by federal communications fiat we were separate. We had to keep the competitive and non-competitive businesses separate because there was fear that we'd use the profits from the non-competitive business [to cross-subsidize competitive businesses].

As top management has reorganized to find the best organizational structure and managerial process, they have tripped and fallen. Perry Colwell discussed AT&T's false starts in attempting to foster intrapreneurialism within its managerial ranks, without concurrently establishing a system of financial control to insure adequate accountability. Perry Colwell's comments also gave testimony to the general lack of experience and preparedness to run competitive enterprises among AT&T's upper middle management:

> When we first divested, there was a movement to push authority and responsibility down the organization. And everybody said, We're coming from this regulated, bureaucratic mindset. Let's set people free. Let's empower lower level

managers. And we did it. Unfortunately it was a time when, because everything changed, we didn't have any financial controls. We allowed too much freedom. We have war stories that will go on forever about some of the horrors we perpetrated . . . We had a lot of people who were involved in the management of businesses that they didn't know anything about, because we had never been in the businesses before. So they weren't coming from years of experience. We didn't have the accountability systems, we didn't have the financial controls . . . Over time, this has settled down significantly. We are beginning to understand those places where we can let people go off on their own. We are beginning to understand what kind of internal controls we need . . . So it's coming along . . . But it still is scary, because I'm not sure we know our way entirely. Since we made mistakes in the early part, there may be some tendency now for overcontrol.

Echoing the concern about overcontrol, Roger Davis discussed the tension between the need for disciplined financial control and the need for informed risk taking in the megadeal competition.

I think it has to do with where the future direction of the business is going and are we properly organized as a management process to win in those opportunities and, then, is the financial organization properly supporting those and in a position to do so? While we organized a certain way to address [market segments], now as we look at where the future is going, how do we make sure that organizational structure serves us for mega-worldwide opportunities? And do we have the right financial processes to support what we've got? [And if not, we must] be prepared to help decide how we have to make changes.

It is within this context of business and organizational change that we wish to discuss the fundamental shift in the mission of AT&T's financial organization. By contrasting the relatively stable, regulated past with the uncertain present and future, we see two fundamentally distinct and different financial function orientations. Virtually every aspect of AT&T's pre-divestiture financial organization is undergoing change, especially in the human resource area.

Changes within the financial organization are being driven by a change in top management expectations. The financial organization must contribute to the formulation and management of competitive strategy. AT&T's top financial management realizes that the move from a regulated to a highly competitive environment requires a change in the role played by the financial staff. The financial professional must change from being an administrator of rules and regulations to being a business financial manager. This role shift is part of AT&T's overall need to change its culture. A culture of financial management is different from a culture of regulatory administration. A financial management culture demands a qualitatively different contribution from financial personnel. A financial management culture is also populated by individuals who have a different set of skills and have a radically different mindset from an administrator. It is this role shift and the accompanying change in the pattern of investment in and management of the financial function that we wish to develop more fully in the AT&T story.

Downsizing the Financial Function: Consolidating Financial Organizations and Systems

Upon divestiture, AT&T realized that the bureaucracy which administered the rules and regulations required by federal, state and local commissions was just not viable in a highly competitive marketplace. As Pete Rhinehart, Corporate Vice President for Taxes, explained:

> We found ourselves considerably larger than what the revenue stream called for out of divestiture.

The realities of a reduced revenue stream required AT&T to make immediate and substantial head count reductions in all administrative areas. These reductions were effected through outright layoffs and through the consolidation of financial activities previously duplicated throughout the firm under the pre-divestiture functional structure.

The downsizing process began in earnest in October, 1986, when the FCC decreed that AT&T could consolidate the regulated and non-regulated sides of its business. Much like Ford did in the early '80s, AT&T took some rather drastic steps. Between October, 1986 and April, 1987, fully one-third of the upper and middle management levels of the financial organization was laid off. Treasury, tax, accounting, and financial systems were pulled out of the functional units and consolidated at the corporate level. After the FCC decree, the now redundant and costly separate financial operations were obvious drains from the revenue stream.

For a firm that had never had to lay off employees, the initial downsizing was extremely painful. During the initial downsizing, AT&T attempted to retain those individuals who could be effective in the new competitive environment. Perry Colwell explained what the downsizing effort meant to the financial organization:

We used the opportunity to increase the level of quality of management in terms of who was going to leave and stay; how we saw them fitting into the future of the organization. As a result, we had to let some people go at higher levels who were okay as current performers. They didn't have the flexibility, mindset, or agility we saw as necessary for the future. That was painful. That was a very conscious strategy: to raise the quality and agility of management.

Larry Prendergast, current Vice President and Treasurer, described the effects of the transformation on the treasury function:

Over the last six years, 50 percent of our managers have left. We went through a transformation that required a new set of skills. People had to accept a new world of competition versus monopoly. People had to develop a new set of skills or leave . . . What you have here, relative to the base, is a set of people who are more flexible, retrainable, willing to be trained to keep up with financial markets. Most of [the former] top treasury people are gone.

In addition to the cuts made at the senior management levels, cuts were also made at the operations level. Between October, 1986 and September, 1988, AT&T reduced financial operations (staff and overall budget) by approximately 20 percent. The financial organization has made a commitment for another 10 percent reduction by the early 1990s. These reductions are being effected through consolidations in developing common financial systems. The dramatic cost savings that have been realized to date underscore the severe fragmentation and redundancy of AT&T's financial systems prior to divestiture.

Upon divestiture, these systems actually added to AT&T's competitive disadvantage. The systems were extremely inflexible and actually impeded efforts to restructure the businesses to become competitive. Tom DeMaria, Vice President, Financial Management and Systems, was quite candid about this problem:

Mr. DeMaria: In '86 . . . we had eight or nine general ledger systems. If you were in Technologies you had a system. If you were in Communications, you had a GL. If you were in Information Systems you had another one. Bell Laboratories had another one. Transtech had another one . . . The same thing was true in payroll, in accounts payable, assets accounting. So the new company really started out with an amalgamation of old systems from the old companies . . . [As] we started reorganizing, it became very obvious that you couldn't reorganize very readily because the systems didn't talk to each other. And as soon as you started putting the factory from the old technology unit [Western Electric] into IS . . . you realized that the IS systems didn't handle factory accounting. So that meant that its financial processing must remain in the factory accounting systems technologies and then converted into the IS general ledger.

The fragmented character of AT&T's financial systems extended down through particular functions as well. For instance, in pre-divestiture AT&T, each of some 20 Western Electric manufacturing plants had its own plant accounting system. The fragmentation of AT&T's financial systems is rather graphically illustrated by the fact that up until January of 1987, the lack of integration among AT&T's payroll systems required employees transferring from the Information Systems business group to the Technologies business group to resign from one organization and fill out papers to join the other organization.

Sitting at the Decision Table: Shifting from a Conformance to a Competitive-Team Orientation

Today, talk of downsizing, common financial systems, organization restructuring is commonplace. AT&T is not unique. What is unique at AT&T is the massiveness of the human resource challenge. "Green-eye-shade accountants" must be retrained (or most likely replaced) by financial managers. As Jim Meenan, Vice President and CFO, Communication Services, explained:

> When you try to take a $34 billion company that's been functioning in a regulated environment, with all the mindsets associated with regulation, and convert that company on January 1, 1984, into a competitive business where you have to know product-specific costs and revenues, that's a mammoth job . . . Forget that we didn't have any systems, forget that our systems were broken. . . we didn't have receivables, etc. Forget all of that. That's just a little problem, a small blip out there. In addition, we were faced with a massive culture change. We had a monopoly in the business and suddenly we were entering a very competitive marketplace.

For AT&T this "culture thing" entails the re-orientation of the financial organization for a competitive world. To make it in the "new" culture, an individual will have to become a value-adding participant in the decision-making process. The interviews with the senior financial managers made it very clear that AT&T must move from its conformance orientation of the pre-divestiture past to a competitive-team orientation. The mandate is to change. The management task is to make it happen without rejecting the contributions that previous generations of financial personnel made in a different environment.

Perry Colwell recounted a recent challenge put to AT&T employees by the current CEO to break out of the conformance mindset that was required of "Ma Bell's" children:

Allen (CEO) said to us all, "We're good at doing things right, but what we need to ask ourselves is whether we're doing the right things" . . . And not only if we are doing the right things, but the right things to win in the marketplace. Anything that does not have as its ultimate goal winning the customer is not really important.

Colwell described the conformance mindset as the accepted way of doing anything within AT&T:

Mr. Colwell: That's a change for a lot of people, particularly people who grew up in the old Bell system, where much of what you were to do was set out for you. If you worked in an operating company financial organization, much of what you did was dictated out of AT&T, out of 195 Broadway.

Interviewer: So you didn't question it because you didn't have much to say about it anyway. So you got into this mode of doing it. Now with a more dynamic market, that mentality just isn't going to cut it.

Mr. Colwell: That's right.

From an employee's perspective, conformity that was expected by external regulators was just internalized and passed on by AT&T managers. Bernie Ragland, Chief Accountant, argued that the single most negative cost associated with regulation is not the specific dollar outlay required to maintain the complex fiscal accountability system; the most negative cost is the "conformance mentality that regulation breeds." Ragland argued that this effect of regulation is particularly insidious because it is pervasive, and over time, becomes an habitual pattern of behavior that, even when recognized, is not easily broken:

Mr. Ragland: If some large percentage of your people get a mindset at the gut level—even if they would see that it was wrong if you could bring it to the intellectual level—they may still behave in certain ways and it may be very hard to change. And that's the greatest drawback to that [regulation], in my judgement . . . What I really mean is that if you get some decision, you have to follow it, you argue about it, you put it into place. Now you cause people not to think about doing things. And therefore it's a very perverse type of behavior pattern, not at the intellectual level at all. It's almost a sin of omission rather than commission . . .

Interviewer: It's the type of thing where . . . if you're basically told what to do by the federal government you don't have to think about what to do . . . whereas as

you enter into a competitive environment you have to get into the mode of thinking about what to do because if you don't, you're going to get nailed . . . you kind
of get lulled by a regulatory environment . . .

Mr. Ragland: Yes. And, as a result of that, you become, in effect, desensitized to
some area you ought to be highly sensitive to. So this is a constant fight, and any
constant fight requires resources. How you quantify those I don't know, but this
certainly is a fallout impact [of regulation] . . . What happens is that you begin to
permeate people's thinking or non-thinking the way I've described. And then . . . it
permeates your systems. And you probably know enough about systems to know
that if you get something starting to permeate a mainframe, it's hard to unpermeate
it. Because now it's a costly thing to go back and redo it, particularly if it's anything
fundamental to the process. So these things are almost indirect in both cases. They
are very real; I don't mean to minimize them. But not the direct thing that you probably think that they are . . .

The current top management group has grown up in the conformance environment that they now are attempting to change. They
have conformed when it was advantageous to do so; they must now
compete because the game has changed. Jim Meenan, who remembers
AT&T's past, talked about "getting ready for the competitive world:"

I'm going to set aside the fact that we are constantly reorganizing the business,
and all I'm going to talk about is what it takes to bring a financial team together to
get them ready for the competitive world. We never had to bid before . . . all we
had to do was sit back and take the orders.

I believe the most important issue facing the financial community at AT&T is
completing our financial placement, both in terms of placing the proper financial
people and the appropriate emphasis, in every single business unit in AT&T.

The regulated world looks at its financial people as "green-eyeshade accountants." Financial people within a regulated world are seen in two ways: First, look
at your best people and make one of them your treasurer because you have to
raise cash. Next, take a look at your most polished people and have them deal
with commissions...and then, find some poor clods to handle the accounting.

If you dealt with any utility, you didn't see a lot of dynamic financial people in its
accounting organization . . . the accounting people "just do your accounting and
let the rest of us run the business."

Given the major image problem that the past has placed on
prospects for the future, getting the right people to put in the business
units will be a challenge. As Jim Meenan explained:

You've got to earn the right to sit at the decision making table with the business managers. They have to see a value added or they simply will not pay attention to you.

I personally don't think we can exist in a competitive environment unless we have the best financial people, 8s, 9s and 10s [on a 10-point scale] in the business units as an integral part of the decision-making process.

However, there is something of a Catch-22, chicken-or-egg element involved in the transition. Financial leadership cannot be willed into existence. Given the historically low level of involvement of the financial organization in the decision-making process, AT&T faces a shortage of staff who possess the capability to make value-added contributions.

Jim Meenan likens the AT&T situation to having to fight a war with untrained soldiers. The financial organization is being asked to put seasoned professionals on the front line to provide financial leadership, but most of the troops haven't finished boot camp:

But we are at war at the time we're making these changes. It's like we're back in boot camp . . . we've just arrived for the first day of training, but we have to take these trainees out to fight the war because we're getting killed.

Watts 800, and private line are under a significant attack because MCI and Sprint have changed their whole strategy. They have moved away from residential services and have gone after the large business customers. So, we've got our people in boot camp when there's a major war over here [in communication services business].

The challenge is to get financial people who can function as effective CFOs to sit at the decision-making tables, to help make the decisions . . . competitive analysis, cost cutting, determining how to get product-specific costs and revenue . . . CFOs who understand the business.

We have hand-picked some people [who have potential] and we've moved some of these people over, but remember, we're in a war over here. We have to ensure that operations people want them and see the value added and at the same time, we've got to find the right people to fill the jobs. That's a big test for this corporation . . .

The change from a conformance to competitive-team orientation has created a people problem for AT&T. In the post-divestiture era, a conformance mentality is just not appropriate at the management levels within the financial organization. Under the conformance orientation, the financial organization had been largely relegated to performing technical accounting tasks. The financial organization was not involved with the business in any significant way. The only important role the financial organization played was in raising capital, but even this function was largely technical. From a control standpoint, the financial function consisted largely of after-the-fact bookkeeping operations to insure technical compliance with fiscal regulatory constraints. Except for the most senior people, financial staff were not key players in shaping or influencing business decisions at AT&T.

Under the competitive-team model, being a value-adding player who has earned the right to sit at the decision table is the name of the game. The metaphor of the "decision table" is used often at AT&T to convey top management's expectations for involvement and personal contribution. As a full-fledged member of the competitive-management team, the financial person is expected to play an active leadership role in the decision-making process, rather than being relegated to or satisfied with after-the-fact bookkeeping and rule administration.

While this section has documented the fact of transition, it has focused more on history with only passing allusions to the "new" competitive-team orientation. In the remainder of the AT&T story, the key themes of leadership, sophistication and accountability that characterize AT&T's brand of competitive-team will be developed.

The Financial Professional as a Team Player: Leadership and Involvement in Shaping Competitive Strategy

An outsider might be tempted to downplay the magnitude and significance of the shift from technical accountant to financial professional. But it is neither mere rhetoric, nor the outcroppings of wishful thinking on the part of financial executives desirous of more power and prestige in the new AT&T. First, financial measurements in the form of financial targets and management performance evaluations, are more important in a competitive environment. In fact, AT&T's financial organization has the primary responsibility for creating the measurement system to support management decision-making.

Based on the Ford, Merck, Citicorp, and 3M experiences, global competition creates a demand for sophisticated financial services. The financial organization must meet the demand or the business managers will go elsewhere to satisfy their needs. Simply put, AT&T is at risk if it does not bring financial professionals to the decision table who can provide leadership in the formulation and management of competitive strategy. That leadership capacity must be grounded in a sound understanding of the "real economics" of AT&T's markets. The stakes are simply too high to not bring the most knowledgeable and sophisticated financial analysis to the decision table.

Concrete evidence of this demand is contained in a set of videotapes produced for use in the retraining of middle managers within AT&T's financial organization. This set of videotapes contains brief statements by each of AT&T's major line of business managers stating their expectations of the financial organization. These tapes were produced to make explicit line management's demand for a different, more involved financial organization.

The tapes communicate very clearly that the model of the "green-eyeshade accountant" is no longer viable, nor appropriate. On one tape, the President of AT&T's Network Systems emphasizes that financial people "are more than bean counters," that the financial organization is "a full member of the management team," involved in "every step of the way" and that the profitability of AT&T depends on the success of the symbolic "handshake process" between the financial organization and line management. The handshake symbolizes the financial organization's "responsibility for translating (line management's performance) commitments into financial reality."

This notion of translation seems to retain an after-the-fact involvement of the financial organization in the decision-making process. However, in elaborating on this role, this same individual emphasized that the financial organization "not only tracks, but shapes commitment." These types of expectations cannot be fulfilled by "green-eyeshade clods."

Another speaker, the President of the General Markets Group (GMG), stressed that everyone in his organization "must understand the financial implications of each (business) decision," that all must "think like shareholders." Thus, he talked of the need for the "counsel of financial professionals to understand the real economics of the business." He stressed the importance of the decision process being "financially driven," which in turn, "requires good financial data translated across organizational lines." This last reference corresponds to the demand for integrated financial information and decision-making alluded to in the previous section. The GMG President called for a two-way learning process involving the financial education of line managers, and the business education of financial managers. He ended by stressing that "no factor is more critical to success than teamwork."

Again, these statements convey an image of a financial professional that stands in stark contrast to that of the green-eyeshade accountant. They indicate a business need for professionals who can help line management understand the real economics and financial implications of each and every business decision. Since every decision is "financially driven," financial managers must understand their business markets and business operations.

The President of the Business Markets Group (BMG) also stressed the need for a "professional financial group" attentive to the need for control and integrity of the decisions and numbers; but he also expressed concern that the business not get bogged down in rigid and complex systems of control, that the financial control system permit "flexibility for change." The President of BMG stressed the leadership role of the financial organization as "a part of the team," "the quality of [its] vision of what AT&T could be" and its plan to "help us get there."

The common themes stressed in these videotapes tell us something about the shift in orientation that top management is trying to orchestrate. The themes that receive the most stress are indicative of the areas most in need of change. In his own way, each of these three leaders stressed:

1) The need financial professionals; who

2) function as value-adding partners in the formulation and management of competitive strategy; where

3) their primary contribution is that of bringing an understanding of the real economics to the decision table.

These three themes echo throughout the interviews conducted with financial executives at AT&T. Together they comprise the elements that define the competitive-team orientation at AT&T.

Of the three themes, the third theme best embodies AT&T's vision of the competitive-team orientation and the problems the financial organization faces in moving away from the conformance orientation. The terms "real economics" and "decision table" seem to be covers for several related issues. Throughout the AT&T story, interviewees have used the decision table metaphor to emphasize the need to become more sophisticated, team-oriented, financial professionals.

The "real economics" of the business is another common AT&T phrase that was used by interviewees to convey a new focus and mission of the financial organization. Thus, the use of the term "real economics" by the President of the General Markets Group, symbolized the need for a high caliber, professional organization. In the following section, we will develop the "real economics" theme more fully.

Bringing the Real Economics of the Business to the Decision Table

From a practical perspective, it is difficult to know the "real economics" of the business without historical financial data to base competitive decisions upon. Prior to divestiture, financial systems were not designed to provide information for competitive analysis. Roger Davis explained AT&T's dilemma in the following manner:

> The job of the financial team in a business unit is to provide the financial information the group needs to make good decisions every day. Now, what are the critical things to make that happen? Obviously, if you're in a reorganization mode, you need to be sure that you have a good sense of the real economics of the business, some history on what's been happening with yourselves and with your competitors. You have to be sure that, because of interdependencies among the units of AT&T, that you have a real set of economics for all the cross charging and internal services you're getting.
>
> So there's a very major issue surrounding the quality and the integrity of data, given the fact that AT&T has been in a state of reorganization trying to best address its customers as we've been given additional regulatory freedom, and trying to find our way into what are the most strategic areas to pursue. So I think making sure the data represent the real economics [is important] . . . As you reorganize your pieces and parts, it's a challenge to be sure you put your finger on the real economics [for] both current and historical [performance] of a unit.

Davis uses the term "real economics" in talking about the need for information that 1) can help managers of newly reorganized divisions to understand the economics of their products and markets and 2) help the firm as a whole understand the interdivisional economics of competing for megadeal contracts.

For AT&T, real economic analysis requires a fundamental restructuring of the product-costing system. Jim Meenan uses the term "true economics" to distinguish product specific costs from average costs. Product specific costs are required for competitive pricing. Average costs are required for universal telephone access. An average-cost mentality fits a regulatory environment; a product-cost mentality fits the competitive environment. Jim Meenan explained the difference:

> You have to really understand our heritage, or where we came from. In a regulated business you're rate-of-return structured, and you do a lot of averaging. You average so that the rate payer gets everything they want . . . the same cost in Montana as in New York.
>
> In a competitive marketplace, you have to know your specific costs by products and services, and you have to know what it costs you to deliver those products and services in every market you serve. Because if you don't know, I'll guarantee your competitor knows.
>
> Remember, the Bell system was built on averages, average costing, average pricing. We went from a regulated environment into a competitive business without knowing the true economics of doing business. The financial people must provide the operations team with the data.

The problem of establishing service-specific costs has been particularly vexing for AT&T in long-distance services. Staff resistance to product-specific costing of the long-distance network has been exacerbated by the fact that AT&T's long-distance services continue to be partially regulated. Many staff do not see the need or appropriateness of changing traditional average costing approaches to cost allocation within the network. Bernie Ragland argued that the average costing/product costing debate keeps the regulative mentality alive:

> The basic theory of regulation is, charge everyone the same prices. The theory of competitive markets is, charge anything above marginal costs that will let you get the business. These two theories conflict with each other in every sense of word.

Financial people have not thought in marginal costing terms, and the financial systems were not designed to provide this type of information. Jim Meenan argued that the financial organization needs to take a leadership role in developing product costs to support business strategy:

> We've never had to bid before. All we had to do was to take orders. We still had this thing called the AT&T long-distance network that provides a major portion of

AT&T's revenue . . . the government said we could run our products and services together as long as we can do accounting separation. But to do that, we have to take this regulated "thing" [the long-distance network] apart.

We have to start looking at the long-distance network on a specific product and service basis, What does it cost us for 800 service, long-distance, special long-distance, operator services?

We have to deal with the old mindset, and I keep coming back to our culture because we have never had to run the business this way before. We must convince about 90 percent of the people that it's even possible to break the costs apart. You'll cripple the business, they say. Well, if we don't "cripple" the business and break these costs apart, MCI may cripple us.

That's the mindset we're dealing with. It's the mindset of operations people as well as the financial people.

Inadequate information and entrenched average-cost thinking are not appropriate for a competitive AT&T. Understanding the "real economics" of the business is not simply a cliche at AT&T. Understanding means knowing your product costs. "Real economics" is a cover term for the fundamental shift in the mentality, skills, and information systems that AT&T's financial organization must make in the midst of continuous organizational restructuring designed to become more competitive. Senior financial managers now realize that regulation reinforces a conformance orientation supported by a pattern of financial work that is dysfunctional in a competitive environment. Part of AT&T's culture change must include a shift in mindset: AT&T is no longer a regulated monopoly; AT&T is a competitive business subject to continued regulation. After you determine your product costs, you can always construct averages. You cannot build product specific costs from average costs. The product cost/average cost discussion is just one example of the cultural change that must take place. Technical compliance with rules and regulations is not a value-added activity in a competitive environment. In the AT&T of the future, financial leadership will come from knowing the real economics of the business and bringing that knowledge to the decision table. This is the essence of the shift from the conformance to the competitive-team orientation.

Getting Close to the Customer: Restructuring the Relationship Between the Financial Organization and the Business Units

In moving from a conformance to competitive-team orientation, AT&T is facing the unenviable task of upgrading the qualifications of its people, while reducing total head count. To survive in the short run, drastic cuts have already been made to bring AT&T's overhead costs into line with its competitors. The long-term strategy is to drive the financial organization closer to business operations by decentralizing financial functions into the business units.

The intent is to replace the discipline of regulatory compliance with the discipline of the market. The two most important priorities for the financial organization in this regard are 1) serving the customer (the business units), and 2) letting the customer drive the level of investment in financial services. AT&T is making a definite cultural and structural change in operating philosophy from centralization to decentralization. To put teeth in this operating philosophy, the most talented financial people are being located in the business units and are not being hoarded at corporate headquarters.

Two aspects of placing financial talent in the business units are particularly worth noting. First, a uniform policy has been established for physically locating the financial people with their business units. Second, financial executives have placed the highest priority on placing top quality staff into divisional controllership positions. As noted in the Citicorp story, talented individuals (from a competitive perspective) are scarce commodities in the beginning of the decentralization process. The initial transition has not been easy for AT&T since the financial organization still tries to promote from within rather than recruit externally. Roger Davis described the talent problem in the following manner:

> The other one [factor] has to do with being sure you have highly skilled financial people who understand the operations of the business unit they're in. Without understanding, you won't be very valuable in the way you deploy the financial analysis. [This is] done in part through co-location [which is] a matter of bringing people together. [In the predominance of cases,] financial people were in a particular building, doing a financial job, throwing data over the transom to operations people, and arguing about what the numbers were.

So the way that people got the experience was a combination of taking some very competent financial people and putting them with the group, so that they started to learn. The other one was taking competent people—who were actually doing a lot of the financial functions—out of the [business] groups [and making them members of the financial organization].

You can't have a financial team that doesn't understand the business making commentary on the sales compensation program. Or, how in the world do they know how do a proper lower-of-cost or market calculation if they don't even know the nature of the business, i.e., where the product comes from, where it goes, what's the selling cycle, what's the seasonality. It's hard to understand if you're off in another building.

The financial organization is being driven closer to the business units in a second, very tangible manner. Similar to the Ford story, the business unit managers have been given more authority to make investment and staffing decisions in what is now their financial function. This shift in operating philosophy has not been without problems in the short run. Tom DeMaria, Vice President of Financial Operations and Systems, explained:

. . . We're putting a management process in place that says the business units are really the center; it's not the NOG [Network Operating Group]; it's not the PR group. It's the organization that has the checkbook that should be in control. If the business units are really the profit centers . . . then . . . they must be able to control the costs they get. In the past . . . if a support organization wanted to spend dollars, they'd just go ahead and spend them . . .

The process we have put in place that I absolutely agree with is, "Hey, you've [the business unit] got the checkbook. I'm not a profit center, so if I can't help you make money, then I'm in trouble. The management process is such that business units that have profitability responsibility have to buy into all my costs. Since I'm a provider of service, the business unit should have an option of buying my service from someone else. If I can't provide my service cheaper than outside, I need to look at what I do and if I can't reduce costs, I should close shop.

That's a significant change from when we used to have a corporate monopoly . . . And we ran the company almost . . . from the top down. You had central control of it from the top. Now we're really pushing that responsibility down to business unit controllers, business unit financial officers . . . But if you're really going to push responsibility out into the business units, I think you have to let go of some of the control mechanisms. Otherwise you're saying, It's your business, but I'm going to control everything from up here. I'm not sure everyone completely understands or has agreed to letting go of those strings. This is a big change.

Bernie Ragland, Chief Corporate Accountant, argued that the best place to locate the head count decision is in the organizational units that are closest to the market. Market-based accountability is the best means for controlling the costs of financial work over the long term:

The financial function costs AT&T too much money. We cannot afford the costs of the present financial function. The process that's underway is to drive the financial function as close to operations as we can drive it—to move away from a centralized financial function, or accounting function: First you centralize, clean it up, then push it out to where it would be directly interfacing with operations, so that it would be provided through that relationship with all the incentives to minimize costs . . . so that ultimately you wind up with a very small headquarters oversight type operation, with most of the accounting function being done by the business units themselves.

AT&T is pushing the financial organization "close to the business." AT&T is taking tangible steps toward an operating philosophy of market discipline. As Bernie Ragland put it:

There are firms that do certain accounting for the sake of doing accounting. There are other firms that do accounting because it is going to bring them some value . . . What we need is to permeate the firm with the philosophy that says anybody who doefs not help that revenue stream is unnecessary and should no longer exist. That would eventually drive you to where the you only did accounting that was absolutely essential. And that's the level you ought to be doing.

Thus, change at AT&T is actually a configuration of changes characterized by the drive to be efficient and provide value-added services to the business units. As the quality of service demanded of the financial organization is being increased, the resources (at least the human resources) are being reduced. The financial organization is being asked to deliver more "bang for the buck."

While there appears to be a shared vision among top line and financial managers of a new type of financial professional, the financial manager, the task is to make the vision a reality.

Case Summary and the Conceptual Model

The AT&T story is one of transition between two distinct orientations, conformance and competitive-team. Each orientation embodies a different configuration of financial work. We cannot say that AT&T "fits" into our conceptual model because, like the Ford story, the management interviews at Ford and AT&T helped shape and refine the current version of the conceptual model. As researchers, we have used the interviews to develop a better conceptual model, to get closer to our customers. The following discussion is, therefore, a restatement of our original AT&T interviews with the benefit of hindsight obtained from the Merck, 3M, Boeing, and Citicorp interviews.

The orientation of the financial organization in pre-divestiture AT&T was conformance. As a quasi-public institution, pre-divestiture AT&T was accountable to the public through government regulation. As long as AT&T conformed with the regulations, it could count on a relatively stable and growing revenue stream. Conforming to external rules and regulations was good business. Conformance made sense as long as no one challenged AT&T's right to provide services as a regulated monopoly. MCI and Sprint challenged that right and triggered one of the most extensive organizational changes in American business history.

Under the conformance orientation, the predominant role of the financial organization was that of bookkeeping and the technical administration of a complex set of cost-allocation rules and procedures. Except for the financial executives at the corporate level, particularly in Treasury, the financial organization did not participate in policy making. The financial organization routinely raised capital through the financial markets and supported the rate increase justification process. The legitimacy of the financial organization was based on knowledge of all of the fiscal statutes affecting AT&T.

Like any organization, AT&T is a creature of its past. In AT&T's case, the conformance orientation and related pattern of financial work was a function of sixty years of regulation. The entire organization developed deeply-entrenched ways of seeing and behaving that became institutionalized in bureaucratic systems and procedures. These habitualized patterns of thought and work practices are part of the culture current financial executives have to change in order to be successful global competitors.

Divestiture and deregulation forced AT&T to rethink and reconceptualize the fundamental nature of financial control. Like Ford and Citicorp, a shift in orientation must be accompanied by a change in operating philosophy. AT&T has moved from being disciplined by regulators to being disciplined by customers and competitors in the marketplace. Financially, AT&T operated in a low-risk, stable, resource-flow environment. The current and future environment is more risky and resource flows are more uncertain.

The term "cataclysmic" has been used to describe AT&T's divestiture and the manner in which AT&T has been catapulted into the world of competition. In the post-divestiture period, AT&T now looks to a competitive environment rather than an institutional environment. The mission of the financial organization has had to change to meet the needs of the "new" AT&T. As Jim Meenan put it, "Financial measurement follows management practices." When it was advantageous to conform to external regulators, the financial organization followed by providing bookkeeping and technical administrative services. It is now necessary and, hopefully, advantageous to compete. Thus, the financial organization is now providing financial leadership and financial support to the business units. The changes in the financial organization are reflected throughout the interviews in the recurrent use of the "decision table" image, the emphasis placed on understanding the business, the role of finance in helping management to understand the "real economics" of the business, and the expectation that the financial person must actively help shape the decision process.

Thus, AT&T is changing. No one can question the challenge that AT&T's managers have faced in coping with the precipitous nature of this change. Whether it can change quickly enough is still an open question. Without adequate financial management, it may easily flounder and lose the substantial competitive advantage it started out with upon divestiture.

6
Boeing

The story of Boeing's financial organization is one of three different cultures existing within the same firm. Partly because of changes in the business environment, and partly because of the very different nature of Boeing's military and commercial businesses, the financial organization has a less unified culture than the financial organizations at the other five firms. Boeing's financial organization cannot be portrayed through a single story. Three separate "short" stories must be told to understand the current financial organization. The orientation of the corporate financial organization differs in significant ways from the orientations of the business units. At the business unit level, there are clear differences between the financial organizations on the military and commercial sides of Boeing. In fact, Boeing was asked to participate in the study primarily because of its mix of commercial and government business. From a research perspective, we wanted to see if the investment in the financial function differed on the commercial and military sides of Boeing. We found the answer to our question to be a resounding "yes," but not for just the reasons one might expect.

From a cost perspective, the military side requires approximately three times the administrative staffing as the commercial side. This increased cost differential is a function of different business environments, different business strategies, different operating philosophies, and different management structures. On the one hand, most people would probably not be surprised to learn that more financial resources must be dedicated to compliance work on the military side to meet the contractual regulatory requirements. On the other hand, it might be more surprising to learn that Boeing's aerospace division also invests more resources than the commercial division to support a highly decentralized, project-oriented management operating style and organizational structure.

The commercial and military stories are also stories of changes within the financial function. The commercial and military sides of Boeing are evolving toward the competitive-team orientation and configuration of financial work. The commercial division is evolving from a command-and-control orientation to a competitive-team orientation. The military division is evolving from a conformance orientation to competitive-team. Changes in both divisions are being triggered by the need to be more responsive in increasingly competitive environments. The controllers within each division are having to rethink their financial control philosophies. The corporate financial organization, on the other hand, seems to exist between a command-and-control orientation and a conformance orientation. The corporate financial organization is oriented toward the efficient use of corporate resources and compliance with defense contract rules and regulations. The corporate group emphasizes oversight to insure that its stewardship responsibilities are fulfilled.

Under the "design-to-cost" and "design-to-build" concepts, Boeing's commercial division is experimenting with team-oriented work processes that challenge the traditional conceptions of the cost accounting or cost analyst roles within the financial function. In fact, Boeing is talking to Ford about its team-oriented operating philosophy and Ford's efforts to streamline its financial organization. If Ford's formula for success could be applied at Boeing, significant cost reductions could result through systems simplification and the elimination of unnecessary head count. The interviews on the commercial side of Boeing suggest that the financial organization is just starting to move in Ford's direction.

In the military side of the house, more tangible evidence of change exists. For example, the aerospace division has scheduled over 20,000 hours of computer training annually for the financial staff in order to move more quickly toward its vision of the new financial professional at Boeing.

Like the other firms in this study, Boeing is a creature of its past. The taken-for-grantedness of institutionalized work practices can get in the way of seeing how things might be done differently. It often takes a major crisis to know that the organization should even be looking. With almost a ten-year backlog of orders on the commercial side, Boeing is in a position much like Merck and Citicorp. The question is whether Boeing can make the changes management believes have to be made without the benefit of a crisis. If a crisis is needed, Boeing should look to Ford and AT&T for guidance on how to change.

The Boeing stories document difference and change, with more emphasis given to difference in the financial organizations. In documenting the differences in financial work between two divisions of Boeing and the corporate organization, this case demonstrates that diversity can exist within the function. The financial organization need not, and possibly should not, be the same across very different businesses. Individual business units facing different business environments, and operating under different operating philosophies and competitive strategies may need to organize financial work differently. While different approaches to organizing financial work can add to the complexity of managing the function at the corporate level, variation provides a context for learning how to do things differently.

Corporate Oversight:
Between Command-and-Control and Conformance

Even though the commercial and military sides of the company have substantially different business management philosophies, they are subject to the same corporate oversight. Boeing's corporate group exerts a high degree of control over the development of business strategy and the operating review process. The corporate group is organized to control all policy-making processes. The divisional financial organizations are another matter. On the commercial side, the team orientation is slowly emerging out of management's efforts to institute a more team-oriented production and design process. However, no sense of any fundamental change in how financial work is organized on the commercial side emerged from the interviews.

On the other hand, Boeing is looking to the aerospace organization to provide the role model for a team-oriented financial organization on the military side. The corporate financial group believes that actual changes taking place in aerospace may eventually work their way over the wall to the commercial side. However, as interview comments clearly point out, the commercial side of the business is radically different from the military side of the business.

As we see in the Ford case, strong corporate oversight is a logical, though not inevitable, result of a highly cyclical and capital-intensive business. The historically cyclical and risky nature of Boeing's commercial business is well-documented. Equally well-known is what *Fortune* has called Boeing's "penchant for high stakes gambling" (Labich, 1987). After World War II, Boeing bet big in pioneering the use of jet aircraft for commercial use. As recently as the late 1970s, more than the entire net worth of the company was committed to launching the 757 and the 767 aircraft. Military projects, although smaller in scope, are equally cyclical and risky thus contributing to the strong oversight role of the corporate group. With that type of high stakes investment, it is not surprising that oversight would be the predominant orientation of the corporate financial function.

Boeing does not really use the language of enforcement as much as it uses the language of stewardship. The corporate group worries about the use of corporate assets. And, as mentioned previously, the corporate financial group works at the top of the hierarchical structure to insure compliance with corporate policies. For instance, the corporate financial group conducts its own reviews of business plans and operations, independent from the reviews conducted by line management. Boeing's review process is reminiscent of Ford's review process in the old command-and-control days.

Although the Ford, AT&T, Citicorp, and to a lesser extent, the Merck stories suggest movement toward a competitive-team orientation, Boeing is clearly not in the same position. Corporate financial oversight is still very prominent in Boeing. Going back to the Ford story, the case for oversight can be grounded in the high risk, high investment nature of the business. The case against strong corporate oversight is that oversight can turn into reduced profits because oversight is expensive and has a negative impact on motivation.

Whether strong corporate oversight helps or hinders the businesses, the fact remains that the corporation owns and allocates the assets. Art Lowell, Vice President and Controller, discussed the need for strong corporate control as well as the "difficulty" it causes in establishing true market-based performance incentives at the division level:

> They [the businesses] do not have autonomy in determining their own destiny. That is why we do not use ROA as a measure. It is hard to use if you are not in charge of your capital, new business expenditures, and how you bid and price your product.

> The divisions are evaluated as quasi-profit centers. They do not have final voice on the capital they spend, how much new business money they spend, key people they need or want. They operate in corporate facilities. They have no treasury.

Part of the problem is the corporate role in deciding who has what resources, who gets what capital, who gets what new business funds and so forth. And we do not want to give up the control we have, but we want to struggle and search for some long-range measure [of success].

In addition to corporate ownership, the corporate group controls the business planning and review process. In terms of our conceptual model, the corporate group's legitimacy is based on its position in the organizational hierarchy as an independent arm of top management. Even though divisional controllers have a solid-line reporting relationship to their division line managers and dotted-line responsibility to the corporate controller, the dotted-line relationship is very strong. While divisional controllers exercise a great deal of discretion over their own operations, there is a high degree of accountability to the corporate controller. Information flows up and down the financial hierarchy independent of the business flows. Art Lowell explained the corporate group's role in the review process:

Guidelines are provided by the finance function for just about everything. There is a location-by-location review by top management at the site. It is a key element of review by the executive council.

A proposal going out has to go to corporate for approval. Any and all exceptions are reviewed at corporate. The controller reviews a lot of proposals. The controller and legal can agree to approve some proposals and not send others to the Board.

Boeing limits the dissemination of restrictive financial information. Corporate planning only gets the financial information that the controller wants it to have. Most of the time, the emphasis is on profit, cash, and cost to completion. All parts of the plan are quantified in dollars and given a subjective difficulty factor—the more difficult the target, the more the incentive dollars are available if they achieve their target.

People out in the field wear two hats; they need to help the divisional president meet his goals and objectives, and they have to give an independent financial review that doesn't need to go through the divisional president. He skates on thin ice.

Dotted- and solid-line relationships are well understood at Boeing. Solid-line is for pay, performance, evaluation, and movement of people. Dotted-line is for policy.

The division finance guy supports the division VP, but sends an independent conservative forecast to the controller. His career is over if he does not do his job. Line management always makes its report to the management council. The board requires a financial assessment quarterly.

If the Boeing case did not consist of three short stories, the corporate story would suggest that there was no movement toward a decentralized competitive-team orientation. As Art Lowell explained:

> Corporate management is getting more and more involved in planning. The former CEO left both sides of the house alone. The big decisions were still made at corporate. Now only decisions over $100 million must be reviewed by corporate. Capital review starts at $200,000. Most decision prerogatives are still kept at corporate.

From Art Lowell's perspective, Boeing has a very traditional corporate financial organization. We must now go into the divisions to get a different view of Boeing. The division controllers are closer to the customer and have a somewhat different view of what their financial organizations are all about. We will start with the commercial story.

The Commercial Story

When we are dealing with the commercial side of Boeing, the complexity and competitiveness of the aircraft business surfaces immediately. Boeing is highly vocal about the skewness of the playing field upon which it must compete against Airbus. Pricing against a government-subsidized competitor, Airbus, has created a new imperative for the entire commercial organization. Management now realizes that product design and manufacturing have to be fully integrated to achieve operating efficiencies. Under this efficiency mandate, the financial organization has been charged with the responsibility of finding ways to reduce the cost of producing an aircraft by over 25 percent. The controller of the commercial division knows that the 25 percent cost reduction objective cannot be achieved without radically changing current financial work practices.

Boeing has a well-established reputation for product quality and service to its customers, but there is a heightened sense in the firm that it must move from being a technology-driven to a market-driven company, especially with respect to the product development process. This new thrust is driven by the increasingly cost-competitive nature of the commercial aircraft business. As a result of greater price competition, Boeing must drive down the cost of bringing new products to market to make a reasonable return. The following comments by various interviewees are indicative of the new imperative. According to Gayle Littleton, Assistant Controller:

Each new product has to compete with all the other products already in the marketplace. The price per seat, operating cost per seat, range, speed, etc., all are extremely important competitive factors to a successful program. New technologies, which are normally required to make improvements, usually cost more to produce. The resultant cost/price squeeze forces the manufacturer to take more stringent measures to control costs.

Wil Loeken, Vice President Finance for Boeing Commercial Airplanes (BCA), emphasized the need to reduce costs in BCA through process improvements:

> You need to get the cheaper process to begin with. Planes take four years for development with a twenty-year product life cycle. The customer does not give a damn what your costs are. Customers think a stretched airplane should be lower. Basically the price is divorced from our cost from the customer's standpoint.

In today's environment, Boeing must continue to move down the manufacturing learning curve to reduce costs. However, the additional 25 percent cost savings must come from product development and product simplification efforts. Wil Loeken talked about the cost reduction efforts:

> Boeing has done a good job of reducing direct cost. However, less than 25 percent of the cost of building a plane is represented by direct labor; therefore, we cannot meet our cost reduction objectives by limiting our activities to the direct labor areas.

Boeing's efforts to develop design-to-build and design-to-cost teams entail a radical change in the entire mentality of the organization. Market effectiveness as well as technical excellence are criteria for success. As Wil Loeken explained:

> In the past, it was design for technical excellence. The design was tossed to the manufacturing people to build. If it could not be built, it went back to design. On the 7J7, it started with the question of what price the airplane can command in the marketplace. Trades are made between weight and costs.

> Boeing slipped after the 727; on the 737 and 747, cost really took a back seat. The work on the 7J7 went beyond the work on the 727. The design has to meet weight, technical, and cost considerations. The cost objective was given equal weight. Recycling occurred when the cost objectives were not met.

> Support of the design-to-cost teams is a significant change at the Commercial Airplane Division. Closing the cost-price loop has greater importance than in the past. We look at the stream of revenue to see if a technological improvement can give Boeing an appropriate return and meet the customer's needs and pocketbook.

How does the technology earn its way onto the product? The engineers are enthusiastic about the process. They are now judged on closing the cost-price loop as well as technical excellence. There is just more emphasis on cost-price relationships now.

A new market-driven approach to product design differs from past practices in terms of the organization of the workplace as well as in giving cost considerations a higher priority. Like Ford and many other American firms, Boeing has emphasized increased technical specialization within a functional organization in the design of the workplace. From lessons learned in competing with Japanese automakers, Ford has just begun to realize that over-specialization creates coordination problems and erects barriers to communication. The Ford story provides ample evidence that over-specialization has had a negative effect on product quality and workplace efficiency. As Boeing tries to eliminate overhead from its cost base, management is experimenting with new forms of team-oriented workplace organization under the concept of design-to-cost and design-to-build themes.

Boeing seems to suffer from the same type of organizational "chimney" problem that Ford had to eliminate in making the shift to the competitive-team model. In Boeing's case "fences" take the place of chimneys. Gayle Littleton, Assistant Controller, alluded, with some poetic license, to the organizational barriers between engineering, materials acquisition, and manufacturing.

> Each organization typically wants more time to accomplish its task than the schedule allows. Without good communication and control between engineering, materiel, and manufacturing, excess up-front flow times result in lots of factory out-of-sequence work and possibly late deliveries.

Design-to-build is one way in which Boeing is trying to find a solution to its internal coordination and communications problems. The BCA financial organization is involved in the design-to-build effort as part of the BCA management team, not as a member of the corporate oversight group. Fundamentally, the job of the commercial business unit is to design and build planes. Once the plane is designed and the price has been set, from a financial perspective, it all comes down to cost control. As Art Lowell explained:

> The divisions are evaluated as quasi-profit centers. The emphasis is on controlling movement down the cost curve. Once the price is set, we go after efficiencies and productivity. The divisions are after a twenty-four month contribution target. Profit contribution is based on price per airplane, offset by cost per airplane and by new product development cost.

Thus, the primary focus of the BCA financial organization is cost control. In fact, the majority of BCA financial staff are involved in some form of cost accounting, cost analysis, or cost estimation. The fact that Boeing makes hard and fast distinctions among these three categories of cost control only reemphasizes the role that technical and functional specialization plays at Boeing.

At Boeing, cost accountants maintain the cost allocation and cost accumulation systems. Cost analysts monitor and analyze costs against budgets for products and organizational units. Cost estimators estimate all costs associated with new product designs, design changes, and customer customization requests. Almost 70 percent of the financial function head count are involved in cost and inventory control.

Under a technology-centered product design philosophy and process, the responsibility of the financial organization was to pick up the ball after the design engineers finished their work. Art Lowell located the tail-end involvement of the financial organization rather succinctly:

> The design decision precedes the capital requirements. The finance people have practically zero input. Design requirements take precedence.

Two results follow from this after-the-fact involvement. The only leverage the financial organization has in cost control is through 1) the power of the veto over certain design specifications on the basis of cost, and 2) monitoring the movement of costs down the learning curve.

The power of the veto over product design is consistent with a traditional command-and-control model. The financial organization provides an independent financial assessment of the viability of the business unit plans. Gayle Littleton described the traditional role of the BCA finance organization in the following manner:

> The financial function maintains all price oversight to keep the functions within limits. The focus is on what you need to do versus what you like to do.

This is not an team-oriented posture. This traditional role for the financial organization is inconsistent with the design-to-build and design-to-cost philosophy. "To get it right the first time" in order to reduce product development time and product costs, Boeing has reconfigured its design process around teams that include design engineers, manufacturing people, and finance staff. The 7J7 program pioneered this new philosophy and role for the finance staff. As Wil Loeken, BCA Vice President Finance, explained:

Price comes from the marketplace; costs must be sufficiently low to produce an acceptable return on investment. The engineer must determine what could be done differently to hit the cost objective. What is different now is the finance function person is right there to help the engineer.

Under this philosophy, finance staff are integral members of the design team. Their job is to insure that the engineers have the necessary information to incorporate the cost perspective into the product design. This is the essence of a market-driven operating philosophy. If the engineers are expected to incorporate the cost dimension into the design process, the finance person cannot function as an independent agent overseeing the design process. The financial person must establish a working relationship with the engineers. In the terms of our conceptual model, this entails a shift from oversight and review to service and involvement, from a command-and-control orientation to a competitive-team orientation. And, according to Wil Loeken, this is precisely the shift that is occurring at BCA:

The financial function person is a respected member of the design to build teams by providing cost data. In the past, it was design for technical excellence only.

In moving to a design-to-cost philosophy, cost control is established at the front-end (upstream) versus the back-end (downstream). Product costs drop as a result of the product simplification process. Again Wil Loeken stressed the difference between the old and new way of doing things:

Design-to-cost is different than cost estimating. If you really work the quality right the first time, you can take 25 percent out of the cost of the product.

The push is really to look at what you are doing. Does it have to be done? Then, do it more efficiently. But do not do it if it does not add product value.

"Getting it right the first time" minimizes the need for engineering changes which wreak havoc on the efficiency of the manufacturing process. "Getting it right the first time" is a significant strategy for minimizing the costs of manufacturing the product:

Learning curves in our business are so powerful. When you make a change, you go back up that curve, which is expensive.

Wil Loeken's comments suggest that changes are occurring within BAC. The design-to-cost philosophy could have a significant impact on how Boeing's top management views cost control. As Boeing moves to a market-driven design process, and the cost perspective is driven down into the engineering process, the financial organization is moving from oversight to involvement. While this is the trend, it is by no means "a done deal." Old habits die hard and the corporate financial organization still operates between command-and-control and conformance. For instance, successful as it has been in winning business, Boeing is now experiencing difficulty in meeting production schedules. In this environment, cost control takes a backseat to scheduling and quality. The financial organization is, in a sense, caught between price competition on the one side and production target pressures on the other side. Wil Loeken explained:

> In order to compete effectively with a heavily subsidized foreign competitor, we have to drive 25 percent of the cost out of the product over and above the learning curve effect. The financial function has to bring to bear financial pressure on the types of targets that are going to be established.

> On some programs, the push for cost control is taking a backseat to meeting production targets. Right now the general manager of the 747 program is worried about parts shortages, maintaining schedule, and meeting the quality objectives of the product going out the door. The GM is not worried about driving things to a new cost level.

> Boeing is trying to change its culture. Some real significant improvements have to be made. How do you get the sense of urgency communicated? At Ford, the need was there. But Boeing has the largest backlog in its history and is building backlog all the time.

The story of the financial organization on the commercial side is one of potential change toward a competitive-team model. However, the current organization is strongly influenced by the command-and-control orientation emanating from the corporate level.

In the next section, the story of financial organization on the military side will tell of similar movements toward competitive-team orientation.

The Military Story

Possibly the most striking feature of the financial function at Boeing is the extent of the differences among the three financial organizations (corporate, commercial, and military). Setting the corporate organization aside for the moment, the commercial and military sides of Boeing differ with respect to 1) the competitive versus the governmental environment, 2) business strategy, 3) management operating philosophy, and 4) organizational structure. Yet, even in the midst of these differences, the military side and the commercial side emphasize effective cost management as their contributions to a competitive-team orientation and configuration of financial work.

The cost-based nature of military contracting forces the financial organization into a position of strategic importance. Poor financial information can lead to poor decisions in the competitive bidding process. The results could be disastrous. Gordon Jorgenson, Controller for Boeing Aerospace (BA), explained:

> The government side has a more complex accounting system. In a military operation, your bid is cost-based. We want to come as close as possible to "true" cost in our accounting practice. In that way you win what you should win and lose what you should lose. And, you do not win those that cost you more to produce than you book in the accounting system.

> All military work is cost-based. The key is the competition and the initial investment that needs to be made. Cost control is needed to live within certain bounds. You must follow the plan, it is all-encompassing. That's important to keep you from losing after you have won.

> You will win, win, win in the areas you are undercosting and lose, lose, lose in the areas you are overcosting. The accounting system then drives you into product areas being favored by the accounting system. It is a natural result of the government procurement process, since the price that you are allowed is based on your cost. This is the reason it is very important for the accounting system to provide as close to true costs as can be effectively achieved. This is not so on the commercial side, where the prices are market-driven.

The risk of exposure to significant audit exceptions also drives the cost accounting intensiveness on the military side. Corwin Lott, General Auditor at the corporate level, explained:

> Under the military side you need to maintain extensive records forever for quality control. You have to establish a modus operandi within an operation and follow it religiously 100 percent of the time.

On the military side, Boeing has to control costs and strictly conform to military contract requirements. Yet, we would argue that, based on the interviews, the military side is shifting from a conformance orientation to a competitive-team orientation.

The financial organization on the military side is reorienting its efforts away from solely insuring technical compliance with contractual requirements to becoming members of the program management and project teams. Corwin Lott's internal auditing group, which reports to Art Lowell, the Corporate Controller, has taken on increased responsibility for insuring compliance with government regulations. The importance and visibility of the internal auditing function adds the conformance orientation to the already strong command-and-control orientation of the corporate financial organization. By moving conformance responsibilities up the organization, the military controllers can concentrate on becoming team members.

Within the military side, Boeing Aerospace (BA) represents the most clear embodiment of the competitive-team orientation. BA's financial organization has been designated as the role model for the other seven separate military business units. As a role model, Boeing Aerospace is the furthest out on the leading-edge of innovation within the military side of the business. From a research perspective, we also believe that other firm's in the defense industry can benefit from learning about the changes this financial organization has undertaken.

Within Boeing, Boeing Aerospace also presents the sharpest contrasts to the commercial side of the business. The fundamental organizational structure and management operating philosophy of Boeing Aerospace are dramatically different from that of Boeing Commercial Airplanes (BCA). Where BCA has ten different operating divisions, BA has 40 distinct programs and 2,400 contracts.

With respect to basic operating philosophy, BA has moved to a highly decentralized and entrepreneurial program and project management system. In this sense, Boeing Aerospace is very similar to 3M's entrepreneurial business unit philosophy. The current operating philosophy was precipitated by the increased competitiveness of the defense industry. BA management realized that they must be able to compete on price in addition to product. The decentralized, project-oriented, management philosophy reflects this commitment. BA's operating philosophy includes two key features:

1) An organizational structure designed to promote an entrepreneurial spirit; and

2) Financial staff who are decentralized into and located with their program and project teams.

This organizational structure and staffing pattern allows the program and project managers to aggressively pursue government contracts while insuring tight financial control at the project level. By being close to the business, the financial people can be more effective in evaluating business risks and measuring performance to control costs.

The financial systems in Boeing Aerospace have been designed to support the program/project management orientation. The decentralized financial system adheres to the competitive-team philosophy of moving financial staff and measurement systems as "close to the business" as possible. Gordon Jorgenson dated this change in management philosophy to the time of the defense cutbacks around 1980:

> Contracts are 25 percent cost plus, 35 percent fixed price, and 40 percent flexibly priced. You still have to be the low cost producer. . . The market change to a competitive emphasis started about ten years ago with defense budget cutbacks. It is a more competitive environment.

> Managers are more entrepreneurial now. We [the aerospace controller's group] are going to force the accounting right into your project. If you want to be cheaper, you have to work your own cost. We also got away from the arbitrariness of the budget process. We now manage the smaller pieces better. We trace direct charges to the project.

> Aerospace is unique [throughout Boeing] in its accounting system. Every manager in Aero has a dollar budget—all 2,400 of them. The manager has the ability to determine how to spend the money.

> Today, the project managers are more entrepreneurs who know what their rates of return on their projects are. These people need the right type of support people. They know their sale levels, which is a total change from the past. The whole division management tracks new business.

The objective of "projectizing" the financial systems and moving them as "close to the business" as possible is valued by government customers as much as it is by project teams. As Gordon Jorgenson explained:

> Boeing tries to achieve an association of the costing to the manager to get projectization of even the overhead cost. . .

> The military side is adopting the BA systems. It is are using systems that even BCS [Boeing Computer Systems] is not using. Cost estimating people are projecticized. Everybody faces off with the DCAA [Defense Contract Audit Agency].

There is no doubt that we are more effective in dealing with the government. The government manager enjoys it because he can understand the system. The people are there. It is not an allocation from on high.

Consistent with the competitive-team, "close to the business" philosophy, the controllers view themselves as key members of their management teams who are involved in the formulation of business strategy. Gordon Jorgenson's perception of the role of his financial managers was a far cry from the corporate position:

The financial function is considered to be a prime ingredient in strategic planning. The financial manager is included in all decisions. The product of the financial function is direct input into product line plans and profitability analysis.

As we found in the other organizations in the study, when the finance people are expected to be integral members of the team, the qualifications and skills required for a team member will differ from the qualifications and skills required from traditional financial function people. Certainly this holds for Boeing Aerospace. As the following comments by Gordon Jorgenson indicate, a "bean counter" mentality is making way for a "financial analyst" mentality. Like Citicorp, Boeing Aerospace places a lot of emphasis on the type of people, educational background, and in-house training that must come together to develop a team member:

New recruits need computer capability when they are hired. Aerospace is scheduling 20,000 hours of computer training annually. The training is to make people into analysts instead of bean counters. Boeing is not looking for bean counters. The minicomputers are doing the bean counting.

The new people in estimating are no longer from accounting, from the shop, ex-engineers. We are going after degree people but not necessarily CPA-trained accountants.

BA places a heavy emphasis on computing skills because of its proactive role in systems development. BA has no interest in relying on financial systems that have been developed centrally and maintained by Boeing Computer Systems. Boeing Aerospace now maintains its own highly distributed computer system that services the financial staff located throughout the 40 programs and 2,400 projects. Financial staff members are expected to perform a good deal of end-user computing to support business planning and financial control. To insure adequate skill levels, BA's financial organization is now recruiting entry-level staff with a higher level of computing capability than has been the case in the past. Furthermore, it is devoting a significant amount of resources to train existing staff members:

> Financial systems are more intensive in aerospace. They want distributed services. They are looking for bilateral training—finance and computing. More and more organic computing capability comes from within the finance organization. Dedicated machines using network services to tie it all together.

> There is a change in character with the merging of finance and computer education. It started with the first dedicated computer for estimating. The new people are computer people with computer science degrees with a smattering of business administration and statistics people.

For a financial function described as being rather traditional, it seems that Boeing Aerospace (whose systems are being adopted by other parts of Boeing doing government business) is making fundamental changes in what it expects from the financial organization.

The Commercial/Military Differences

In the previous two sections we have focused mostly on what was going on within each financial organization. In this section, we will focus primarily on some of the significant differences that exist between Boeing Aerospace and Boeing Commercial Airplanes. From the interviews, it became obvious that the two financial organizations differ in operating philosophy and organizational structure as well as in the basic nature of their financial control systems.

Controllers on each side of the house are also very aware of their differences. Some rather stark differences exist in terms of staffing intensity, strategies for systems development, and recruiting and development. We have a situation in which the military and commercial sides of Boeing are being told to move toward common corporate systems and procedures in spite of strong and enduring organizational differences. It remains to be seen whether a corporate philosophy of common systems, procedures, and financial practices will help improve Boeing's bottom line.

When asked if the two sides of Boeing were different, Gordon Jorgenson referred to the more decentralized operating philosophy of Boeing Aerospace in comparison to Boeing Commercial Airplanes:

Oh, yes! We are miles apart as to what is possible. The dollar budget example is an indicator of different philosophies. [Aerospace project managers have dollar budgets, commercial managers do not.] The total philosophies are different. The organizations are different. They have been different for a long time.

Art Lowell reinforces the differences in terms of the measurement system that is used to report the financial performance of the commercial side in the audited financial statements:

The other thing that runs through there is that our financial records and our performance measures, the way we keep our books in finance is totally different for commercial and military. Military is the same as the annual report. On the commercial side, the way we measure performance is totally different from the way we keep our books.

On the commercial side, costs are smoothed on a long-run average-cost basis. This practice is not followed on the military side.

The differences between commercial and military go beyond book-keeping and reflect a basic difference in culture. These cultural differences can be best appreciated by understanding the strong resentment that BCA finance staff have toward governmental accounting procedures.

On the commercial side, government business represents a small part of the action (5 percent), but a disproportionately large part of the costs. Art Lowell, Corporate Controller, has indicated that Boeing will probably stop doing business with the government on the commercial side because the high costs reduce returns. Wil Loeken, BCA Vice President, Finance, explained the nature of the problem in doing business with the government:

The procurement regulations are meant for a product designed for the government. The government will ask for a clause that will let government auditors examine your records. Why does a government auditor have to examine a commercial contract for hundreds of parts just because one part might be used on a new Air Force One or Command Post Airplane? The flow-down requirement for building that part is that the government can audit the whole operation.

Why don't we put all those things [government regulations] into our contracts? We could not stand those expenses in a competitive, commercial environment. You are at risk for years and years into the future. The government can go back many years. They can raise all kinds of nit-picking issues. Since the government is only 5 percent of the business, the added costs go against commercial. BCA has to eat those costs if it wants the president to fly a 747.

> It is extremely difficult to walk the line of being sure that we fulfill all requirements, and yet do not put onerous and meaningless requirements down into our supplier network. These added costs make BCA less competitive on the commercial side.

What is a potentially onerous cost of doing business on the commercial side is a normal cost of doing business on the military side. And what is viewed as distasteful to the commercial financial staff, i.e., dealing with governmental accounting procedures and auditors, is viewed as an intrinsic and inevitable part of the job by military financial staff. As a result, there is little or no movement between the commercial and military sides of the business.

Art Lowell is currently trying to promote greater movement between the commercial and military sides. But he faces the challenge of convincing people that there are lessons to be learned from switching cultures.

Doing Business With the Government: The Costs of Regulation and Adversarial Relations

The differences between the commercial and military sides of Boeing extend beyond mere attitude problems. As the comments by Wil Loeken, Vice President Finance for BCA, clearly indicate, there are significant costs of financial control inherent in doing business with the government. And, these costs are increasing due to the increased adversarial character of defense contracting that has evolved in recent years. We close this case with a discussion of these costs and their significance.

Doing business with the government can be broken down into two basic components 1) managing the high cost of government regulation, and 2) managing the contractual exposure inherent in doing business with the government. With respect to the second component, adversarial relations between the government and contractors create the potential for charges of fraud, waste, and abuse. Insuring compliance with the rules and regulations to protect the organization from being accused of fraud by the Defense Contract Audit Agency (DCAA) can be very expensive.

Since military business is only 5 percent of the commercial revenue stream, it does not make sense to structure the entire organization for government compliance. Gordon Jorgenson compared the costs of financial work on the commercial and military sides:

> The military side is identical to commercial in terms of internal controls for all plans. In addition, the military has monthly customer reports, DCA reports, cost

accounting standard reports, agency reviews, cost accounting disclosure statements. These requirements drive up the costs of investment [in financial work]. The military requirements are drivers.

The costs of conformance must be factored into the contract price. As long as Boeing and other defense contractors do not underestimate their conformance costs, they should not be tempted to cut corners on contractual requirements. The government ultimately pays for the costs of compliance. The increased cost of government business is evidenced, in part, in the higher financial staffing intensity on the military side. As mentioned previously, the military side requires approximately three times the financial staffing as on the commercial side.

But beyond increasing the costs of financial control, government contract requirements thwart efforts to do a better job. As an executive in Boeing's internal audit group put it:

> Internal audit sees the whole company and can communicate good practices from one division to another division, but the legal requirements get in the way of good practices. Legal requirements override efficiency and productivity.

What must be particularly frustrating for organizations like Boeing is having to trade off external accountability for efficiency. When other firms included in this study are moving away from command-and-control and conformance, Boeing cannot escape the adversarial climate of government contracting if it wants to continue to participate in developing state-of-the-art technology.

While it is hard to argue against the need for greater accountability given the recent rash of convictions for fraud in the industry, the costs of external accountability are substantial. Corwin Lott spoke to the relationship between defense contractors and the Defense Contract Audit Agency.

> They took the commas out of fraud, waste, and abuse. It's all fraud.

> In the past, you did not have a significant adversarial relationship [with the DCAA]. It did not lead, in every audit report that they wrote, to a threat to suspend progress payments and/or criminal investigations. If DCAA does not get immediate satisfaction, it moves into these other activities leading to criminal prosecution investigations.

> Exposure to risk, fraud, etc. dictates devoting more resources to the government side [of Boeing]. Today the government attitude has changed. In the old days you could make mistakes and work out the mistakes with the contracting officer. Now, the government says that is fraud. Now, errors in claims are considered to be fraud.

The threat of criminal prosecution and the threat of payment suspensions cannot be taken lightly. To minimize the possibility of being out of compliance with contract requirements, Boeing has substantially beefed-up its internal audit group. The internal audit group has doubled in size over the past three years, with 60 percent of all auditing work devoted to the government side of the business. Certainly this percentage is out of proportion to the revenues generated by government business:

> There has been a 180 degree change. Top management now wants internal auditing there first to minimize the exposure for criminality, suspension, and just the administrative hassle of responding to a DCAA audit report and all that cost . . . There is a lot of exposure, a lot of cost, a lot of effort. Top management wants to keep that kind of stuff to a minimum. The top areas of audit concern are 1) spare parts pricing, 2) labor charging, 3) inventory, MRP, and now 4) product integrity.

> One suspension could cost you millions and millions of dollars. Boeing is very concerned about its reputation. The investment in internal auditing is worth it from top management's perspective.

In less adversarial times, Boeing relied on the DCAA auditors to provide feedback to management concerning the operations which required greater audit attention and oversight. As Corwin Lott explained:

> There are more auditors on the government side because of our exposure. In the past, the philosophy was that if DCAA, GAO, and other government oversight people were there, you did not need as many auditors because you could depend somewhat on their work.

The effects of the adversarial relations are being felt throughout the firm, not just in the military side of the business. From the corporate controller's perspective, the DCAA demand for strict compliance is putting a tremendous amount of pressure on the entire financial organization. Gayle Littleton, Assistant Corporate Controller, talked about the need to document actions through the accounting system.

> Under the post audit award, they look at a proposal. Say you did not have all the data completely up-to-date. They [the DCAA] can make subtractions from your profit. You need a tremendous amount of documentation. You have to be very current on your data, all the details, so that they cannot come back and say "Heh, look, you have a defective pricing claim."

> They do it all the time and its big bucks, millions of dollars that you lose because of defective pricing claims. They find the errors. The burden of proof is on Boe-

ing. They can always find something and they do. As auditors, they are taught to find little faults and screw ups.

In order to meet the DCAA audit requirements, compliance controls must be built into the accounting system. It is no small wonder that Boeing is seriously contemplating the elimination of all governmental contracting on the commercial side of its business. To decide otherwise might be competitive suicide. In fact, when 3M's intention to integrate its commercial and government businesses was mentioned in the interviews, Gordon Jorgenson's advice was "Don't do it; keep the commercial side separate from the government side."

Case Summary and the Conceptual Model

The foregoing analysis has documented the story of Boeing's financial function using the language and concepts of our conceptual model. To reiterate our opening statements, the Boeing story is actually three "short" stories.

The corporate financial organization is a combination of the command-and-control orientation and the conformance orientation. The command-and-control orientation has a long history and tradition at Boeing, and there does not appear to be any desire on the part of corporate management to relinquish any control to the divisions. The conformance orientation has surfaced as a result of the increased adversarial nature of contracting with the government. Boeing has elected to provide significant monitoring of conformance from the corporate level and has increased internal audit efforts on the military side.

The commercial side of Boeing is moving (we think) toward the competitive-team orientation. Top management talks as if they want to emulate Ford's success in changing their entire operating philosophy. The rhetoric of competitive-team, is evident from the interviews. However, with the exception of the design-to-cost experiments, there is little evidence of more substantive change.

The military side of Boeing, as evidenced by the interviews at Boeing Aerospace, is moving more concretely toward the competitive-team model. There has always been a strong conformance orientation associated with government work, but two factors keep the military side from becoming pure conformance. First, the competitive bidding process requires a level of financial sophistication that cannot exist in a "bean counter" environment. Second, the corporate internal auditing group has assumed a larger roll in insuring conformance and compliance. Gordon Jorgenson and the Boeing Aerospace financial organization have been encouraged to continue their pioneering work in moving toward the competitive-team model.

The question is, "Can three very different short stories be integrated into a full length novel?" Can command-and-control, conformance, and competitive-team orientations co-exist over the long run? Within BCA, the potential exists for significant changes in the prevailing patterns of financial work. Will BCA become more like Ford? Within Boeing Aerospace, the financial organization is becoming more computer literate and is highly decentralized. Will Boeing Aerospace become more like a Citicorp?

As the self-expressed most-traditional financial organization included in the study, Boeing has the greatest potential for change, yet it may desire to remain basically the same. At this point, it is not clear what will happen. If it takes an economic crisis to precipitate change, then Boeing is likely to continue on its path of slow evolution to competitive-team. With the backlog that Boeing has built up, an economic crisis is not in the cards in the foreseeable future.

No matter how the financial organizations within Boeing change, they are still part of an organization that was been voted one of America's most admired corporations for 1987 and 1988 in *Fortune Magazine's* annual survey of corporate executives.

Appendix A

Research Design and Methodology

Background

In the beginning, we planned to use a survey research methodology for this study. We assumed that the literature would give us a basis for designing a comprehensive questionnaire for financial executives to fill out concerning the management of the financial function. Then, along with the data from all the firms, we would be able to identify broad, statistically significant patterns of variation and change across a representative sample of firms in corporate America. In theory, the research design seemed workable. But, in practice, we found it was not feasible.

We became more aware of the practical realities when we met with Bob Moore, then Executive Director of the Financial Executives Institute (FEI), and Roland Laing, current Director of Research of the Financial Executives Research Foundation (FERF). Considering the number of surveys that all executives are being bombarded with, the chances of getting an adequate response rate were extremely low.

Even if the response rate problem could be solved, we would be faced with a communications gap. The language of theoretical and empirical academic research is not the language of business. If the terms employed in the questionnaire were too vague or too confusing for the respondents, the research findings would probably have little relevance for the full FEI membership.

Both Bob Moore and Roland Laing felt that financial executives would be more likely to participate in an in-depth study designed to evoke a rich understanding of their own and other firms' financial organizations. If the firms were chosen to represent the composition of the FEI membership and blend elements of similarity and difference into the selection process, financial executives could relate to concrete examples and determine for themselves whether any patterns of variation and change were relevant to their own organizations.

In one sense, the initial meeting with Bob Moore and Roland Laing confirmed the criticisms of survey-based research on organizational functioning. Management theorists such as Mintzberg and Miller (Mintzberg, 1983; Miller, 1981; Mintzberg and Miller, 1983) argue that academic researchers cannot gain an intimate knowledge of the complex dynamic nature of organizations solely through cross-sectional, survey-based research. Research from a distance fails to capture the phenomena it purports to understand. Survey-oriented data must be supplemented with first-hand observation. And first-hand observation means getting out into the field.

We believe that, by using this intimate form of research, we have been able to produce a study that may be of use to financial executives and academic researchers interested in the changing nature of financial management in corporate America.

Research Design

When we adopted the field-based case study design, we were limited in the number of organizations we could study. We settled on six as a feasible number. Technically speaking, we employed a multiple case study design (Yin, 1984). Through such a design, researchers engage simultaneously in description and explanation. In this study, we set out to identify and describe the facts of change, if any, in the financial organizations of the six firms we selected. However, our objective was never to stop at description. We wanted to offer explanations and/or insights as to why these patterns of variation and change were occurring.

In limiting our study to six firms, we were aware that the relevance of the research and the ability to generalize from it depended heavily on which companies we selected. We were also aware of the often justified criticism that case study research lacks rigorous procedures for assessing and reporting on research validity and reliability. As a result, case study write-ups seldom give the reader sufficient basis for distinguishing between the facts of the case and the researchers' interpretation of those facts. When readers cannot judge the plausibility or replicablity of the findings for themselves, the study suffers from a scientific standpoint (Miles and Huberman, 1984; Yin, 1984). With the possibility of such criticism in mind, we have summarized those aspects of the research design that address the issues of validity and ability to generalize.

Selecting the Firms

In selecting the six firms for the study, we used a combination of practical and conceptual criteria. Our first criterion was practical in the sense that we wanted to choose firms with financial organizations that might

serve as exemplars of effective financial management practices in industries representative of FEI membership. FERF is responsible for supporting research studies that provide financial executives with additional
insights into the management of their financial organizations. Furthermore, by studying firms noted for their overall business and financial
success, we believed that we could establish a baseline for evaluating
the criticisms of financial management practices characterized by the
managing-by-the-numbers debate discussed in Chapter 2.

Our second criterion was conceptual and focused on the ability to
generalize from the data. We wished to study firms that maximized our
exposure to the most common and significant sources of variation and
change in the management of the financial function. We took these
potential sources of variation to be 1) the industry in which the firm
competes, 2) the character of the products and services offered by the
firm and the competitive and regulatory environment in which the firm
operates and, 3) evidence of firm-wide strategic adaptation that might
affect the financial function. Finally, we had to select firms that would be
willing to participate.

We then had to decide how much diversity, versus similarity, to build
into the sample. We didn't want to analyze six completely different types
of firms. On the other hand, we didn't want to restrict the study to six
examples of a particular type of firm faced with a somewhat specific set
of financial issues. We were interested in gauging patterns of variation
and change in which each firm shared some characteristics with at least
one other firm in the study.

Details of the selection criteria are shown in Table A.1.The first two
specific criteria deal with the type of industry and type of firm within
industry. The third criterion was used to obtain some degree of similarity
and difference among industries and firms.

Validity

Case studies have been criticized, with justification, for not following
established procedures for assessing and reporting on research validity
and reliability. Part of this criticism centers around the tendency of case
researchers to concentrate on the what-found while failing to document the how-found. This failure leaves the reader without a means to
evaluate the integrity of the research design or the rigor with which the
research was performed. Considering the serious threats to validity that

TABLE A.1   Sample Selection Criteria

1. Select a cross-section of industries that:

    a. Represents major goods and services sectors of the economy.

    b. Exhibit variation in terms of markets, production processes and regulatory environments:
       - Nature of competitive pressure (price, product, distribution)
       - Stability of business cycle
       - Automated production
       - Product development cycle
       - Significant regulatory influence or change in regulatory influence

2. In each of these industries, select firms that are high financial performers and possess one or more of the following characteristics:

    a. Have an established reputation for innovation and/or strong financial management,

    b. Operate in both regulated and non-regulated markets,

    c. Have undertaken strategic adaptations that may affect the financial function.

3. Each firm selected for inclusion in the study should possess a constellation of characteristics that:

    a. Permit comparisons to be made to at least one other firm on at least two separate dimensions—industry, environmental characteristic, firm characteristic, and/or

    b. Permit comparisons to be made to at least two other firms on a single (but possibly different) dimension.

exist in case-oriented studies (Miles and Huberman, 1984; Yin, 1984), more attention must be directed to the how-found part of the research. Case study researchers, in effect, often fail to provide a research audit trail which describes the procedures followed in developing the case. As a result, readers cannot determine whether or not the research can be replicated. In the following paragraphs we describe:

1.   The three phases of the research process.

2.   The data collection principles used to insure validity and reliability.

3.   The research audit trail which links the qualitative and quantitative data to the firms' stories and the conceptual model.

The Research Process

There were three phases in the research process—a subjective phase, an objective phase and an inter-subjective phase.

The Subjective Phase. During the subjective phase of the study, financial executives were asked to respond to a set of questions concerning:

1. Their responsibilities and the key success factors for themselves and the financial organization.

2. The most significant changes affecting the firm's approach to financial management.

3. Any additional specific topics they considered relevant to the study.

The full list of questions appears at the end of this chapter.

Before we conducted the interviews, we gave each participant a copy of the executive summary of the research proposal submitted to FERF. All research interviews were conducted on site and lasted from one to three hours. With one exception, the interviews were tape-recorded, and the taped interviews were used to build the respondent database of coded comments.

In several cases, there were questions about the authorship or wording of a quotation, or questions arose concerning the amount of emphasis devoted to a particular issue raised within a firm. In all instances, participants who raised questions were given a complete listing of their comments coded into the database.

The Objective Phase. During the objective phase of the study, each participating firm completed a questionnaire about the organization of that firm's financial function. We collected each firm's basic demographic data on earnings, assets, returns, employment, etc. In addition, we obtained basic head count and financial data for the last ten years, where available, on typical categories of financial work—accounts payable, general accounting, planning and analysis, etc. These data are not included in the body of the study at the request of the participating firms. But they provided the basis for the quantitative assertions included in the stories—for example, the head count reductions at Ford and 3M.

Even more important than the standard surveys, was the objective data that we discovered during the interview process: such as the Mazda studies at Ford; the Kearney study mentioned at Ford, Merck and 3M, and the management video tapes and related documentation at Merck and AT&T. These internal studies and industry benchmark studies proved to be an invaluable source of data for fleshing out the firm stories.

The Inter-Subjective Phase. During the inter-subjective phase of the study, each firm was asked to review and, if necessary, revise the stories which resulted from the analysis of the data that were collected during the subjective phase of the study. During this phase, respondents saw, for the first time, how we as researchers interpreted their comments within the context of all six firms. For example, respondents at Ford saw for the first time how their individual comments fitted together with the comments of other Ford respondents. All respondents at Ford saw for the first time the Ford story within the context of the other five stories.

During this inter-subjective phase, two major types of adjustments were made or suggested by the participants. First, individual quotes were edited to clean up the conversational style or to correct difficulties encountered in transcription. Second, respondents often suggested wording changes to convey more succinctly the essence of the interviews within the context of the conceptual model. No changes of major conceptual import in the substance of the individual stories or the conceptual model were made. In 3M's case, the relative emphasis of the story was revised giving greater attention to 3M's financial systems.

Data Collection Principles

We used three principles of data collection to lessen the threats to validity inherent in case study research. First, we incorporated the principle of data source triangulation into the study. As described above, we collected subjective and objective data and shared all data with the participants.

Second, we placed particularly strong emphasis on the principle of systematic management and coding of the qualitative interview data. These data formed the basis for telling each of the firm stories and developing the conceptual model. The coded interview comments gave us the basis for identifying the deep structure within the interviews at each firm and across all six firms.

Third, in keeping with the research principles recommended by grounded researchers such as Miles, Huberman, Glaser, and Strauss, we started the coding process with a set of theoretically-generated categories that gradually evolved into a working set of in-vivo categories. which is reflected in Figure 2 in Chapter 4. The construction of the initial codes, and their ongoing modification and analysis, added discipline to the research process and forced us to keep the emerging conceptual model of organization of financial work grounded in the subjective and objective data.

The coding process was shared jointly by the two of us. The initial coding of the AT&T, Ford and Merck interviews was done by one of us, while the other one did the initial coding of the 3M, Boeing and Citicorp interviews. While there was much discussion about how to code the interview data, each of us used his own coding scheme. These schemes were then integrated and merged to create the research database of coded responses. In view of the quasi-independent nature of the coding process, as well as some duplicate coding of the AT&T, Ford and Merck data, we believe that threats to validity stemming from our coding biases were kept to a minimum.

As we become more involved with other firms and financial organizations, we anticipate making modifications to the current coding scheme which will entail reorganizing the individual comments, or data elements, to match the evolution of our knowledge of how the financial function is being managed. In fact, doctoral dissertation research is currently in progress which focuses specifically on developing a more sophisticated, mathematically-based model of the patterns of variation and change within the financial organizations of the six firms included in the study.

Research Audit Trail

We believe a particular strength of this research was the development of a research audit trail of documentation which links the interviews to the stories and the conceptual model. Our audit trail consists of:

1. The recorded tapes.

2. The computerized database of coded interview comments, or data elements.

3. A matrix of interview comments summarized by firm, by categories of the conceptual model.

4. The case studies presented in Section B.

When questions arose concerning the development of a firm's story or how interview comments related to the conceptual model, we were able to give the participants a direct link back to their own comments.

A more extensive description of the research design and methodology, including actual respondent data from the six firms, is currently being prepared to serve as a guide for researchers interested in conducting field-based, case study research.

Questions for the Interviews With Financial Managers

Responsibilities and Key Success Factors

The purpose of the first set of questions is to discuss the factors that influence the level of organizational investment in financial management (dollars, people and technology), and the basic approach to the management and organization of those resources.

1. Please describe, in your own words, the overall responsibilities of your group. To what extent is the nature of your activity driven by industry and firm specific characteristics?

2. Recount briefly the career path you have followed to reach your present position?

3. What are the factors most critical to the success of your operations?

4. How does the operating philosophy of top management generally, and the CFO specifically, most tangibly affect how you manage your operations and the issues on which you and key members of your staff concentrate most?

5. What are the key (most sensitive) interdependencies between your operations and the rest of the organization (within and outside the financial function) that must be managed?

Most Significant Changes

The purpose of this set of questions is to learn about the major changes affecting the firm's approach to financial management. We are particularly interested in identifying the sources and impacts of these changes. For instance, to what extent have these changes been the result of key strategic initiatives or competitive pressures facing the firm as a whole, versus changes the CFO and his staff have initiated in the management of the financial function, independent of firm-wide considerations. We are also interested in determining whether a particular change has affected the amount and/or allocation of resources devoted to specific units of the financial function and in what ways, if any, each change has resulted in new activities, new modes of organization, or broader processes of communication among financial staff.

We would like to know if there have been any significant changes in the specific duties performed or capabilities offered by your unit. If so,

1. Have these changes increased or decreased the resources devoted to your unit, or have they simply changed the internal allocation of resources within the unit?

2. To what extent have these changes been driven by strategic initiatives of the firm? Are these initiatives driven by market, technological, or regulatory changes, or changes in management philosophy?

3. In each case of change, what factors have facilitated or constrained the process of change?

4. Which of these changes have been initiated by you and your staff?

Specific Topics

The following questions pertain to specific topics that should be discussed in the interview with each manager. If these topics have not been discussed in the course of the interview, the following questions are meant to stimulate discussion at this juncture. Each issue should be addressed in terms of its impact on the investment in, the organization of, and the services provided by the financial function.

1. Has cost containment or an emphasis on productivity within the financial function been a significant source of change in the management of your unit? If so, how have you been addressing this matter?

2. Has the theme, "quality of services," been a significant source of change in the management of your unit?

3. Would you say that the role of your unit in the decision-making process has increased, decreased or remained the same in the past five years? In which areas is change most pronounced?

4. It has been asserted that American executives tend to be overly focussed on short range financial objectives. Would you comment on the merit of this assertion? What role does the financial function play in helping top management to balance short and long range financial objectives?

5. How does the global nature of your firm's operation most tangibly affect the nature and scope of your operations?

6. What do you take to be the most significant influence of information technology on your operations?

In Summary

Of all the key issues we have discussed in this interview, what are the two or three most critical ones that have impacted your operations over the past five years?

Bibliography

To assist the reader we have divided the bibliography into two sections. The first section contains the references pertaining to the substance of our study. The section section contains the references pertaining to the research philosophy, design and methods employed in our study.

References on Organization/Management Theories and Practices

American Accounting Association, Committee on the Future Structure, Content, and Scope of Accounting Education (The Bedford Committee) "Future Accounting Education: Preparing for the Expanding Profession," *Issues in Accounting Education* (Spring, 1986): 168–195.

American Management Association, *The Financial Manager's Job* (American Management Association, Inc., 1964).

Argyris, Chris, "Organizational Learning and Management Information Systems," *Accounting, Organizations and Society* (1977): 147–156.

Argyris, Chris and Donald Schon, *Organizational Learning: A Theory of Action Perspective* (Addison-Wesley, 1978).

Arthur, Anderson & Co., Arthur Young, Coopers & Lybrand, Deloitte Haskins & Sells, Ernst & Young, Peat Marwick Main & Co., Price Waterhouse, and Touche Ross (The Big Eight), *Perspectives on Education: Capabilities for Success in the Accounting Profession* (April, 1989).

Ballon, Robert J., and Iwao Tomita, *The Financial Behavior of Japanese Corporations* (Kodansha International, 1988).

Bedford, Norton M., and William G. Shenkir, "Reorienting Accounting Education," *Journal of Accountancy* (August, 1987): 84–91.

Bennett, Earl D., et. al., *Financial Practices in a Computer Integrated Systems Environment* (Financial Executives Research Foundation, 1987).

Bowles, Samuel and Herbert Gintis, *Democracy and Capitalism* (Basic Books, 1986).

Brinberg, David, and Joseph E. McGrath, "A Network of Validity Concepts Within the Research Process," in Brinberg, David, and Louise H. Kidder (eds.), *New Directions for Methodology of Social and Behavioral Science: Forms of Validity in Research* (Jossey-Bass, 1982):5–21.

Brown, W., and K. Montamedi, "Transition at the Top," *California Management Review*, Vol. 20, No. 2 (1977): 67–73.

Burchell, Stuart, Colin Clubb, Anthony Hopwood, and John Hughes, "The Roles of Accounting in Organizations and Society," *Accounting, Organizations and Society* (1980): 5–27.

Burns, Tom, and G. M. Stalker, *The Management of Innovation* (Tavistock Publications, 1961).

Burrell, Gibson, and Morgan, Gareth, *Sociological Paradigms and Organizational Analysis* (Heineman, 1979).

Business Week, "How the Best Get Better, Robert Waterman Follows Up His Research for Excellence," *Business Week* (September, 14, 1987): 98–120.

Business Week, "How the New Math of Productivity Adds Up," *Business Week* (June 6, 1988): 103–114.

Cammann, Cortland, "Effects of the Use of Control Systems," *Accounting, Organizations and Society*, Vol.1, No.4 (1976): 301–313.

Chandler, Alfred D. Jr., and Herman Daems, "Administrative Coordination, Allocation and Monitoring: A Comparative Analysis of the Emergence of Accounting and Organization in the U.S.A. and Europe," *Accounting, Organizations and Society*, Vol.4, No. 1/2 (1979): 3–20.

Child, John, "Parkinson's Progress: Accounting for the Number of Specialists in Organizations," *Administrative Science Quarterly* (1973):

Cooper, Robin, and Robert S. Kaplan, "How Cost Accounting Distorts Product Costs," *Management Accounting* (April, 1988): 20–267.

Davey, Patrick J., *New Patterns in Organizing for Financial Management*, Report No. 839 (The Conference Board, 1983).

Dertouzos, Michael L., Richard K. Lester, and Robert M. Solow, *Made in America: Regaining the Productive Edge* (The MIT Press, 1989).

Dixon, J. Robb, Alfred Nanni, and Thomas E. Vollman, *The New Performance Challenge* (Dow Jones–Irwin, 1990).

Duncan, Robert, and Andrew Weiss, "Organizational Learning: Implications for Organizational Design," in Barry M. Staw and L. L. Cummings (eds.) *Research in Organizational Behavior*, Vol. 1 (JAI Press, 1979): 75–123.

Earle, Michael J., and Hopwood, Anthony G., "From Management Information to Information Management," in H. C. Lucas (ed.), *The Information Systems Environment* (North-FHolland, 1980): 3–13.

Feldman, Martha S., and James G. March, " Information in Organizations as Signal and Symbol," *Administrative Science Quarterly*, Vol. 26 (1981): 171–186.

"Finance Business Plan" (Ford Motor Company, 1988).

Fleming, Richard L., "A Prognosis for the New CFO, Nineteen Critical Concerns That Are Changing the Job," *Financial Executive* (September, 1986): 27–30.

Fligstein, Neil, "The Intraorganizational Power Struggle: Rise of Finance Personnel to Top Leadership in Large Corporations, 1919–1979," *American Sociological Review*, Vol. 52 (February, 1987): 44–58.

Ford Motor Company, Mazda Comparison Study, Phase IIB (Unpublished, April, 1986).

Foster, George, and Charles T. Horngren, "JIT: Cost Accounting and Cost Management Issues," *Management Accounting* (June, 1987): 19–25.

Galbraith, Jay, *Designing Complex Organizations* (Addison-Wesley, 1973).

Geneen Harold S. "The Case for Managing by the Numbers," *Fortune* (October 1, 1984): 78–81.

Gerstner, Louis V. Jr., and M. Helen Anderson, "The Chief Financial Officer as Activist," *Harvard Business Review* (September-October, 1976): 100–106.

Govindarajan, V., and Anil K. Gupta, "Linking Control Systems to Business Unit Strategy: Impact on Performance," *Accounting, Organizations and Society*, Vol.10, No. 1 (1985): 51–66.

Habermas, Jurgen, *Communication and the Evolution of Society* (Beacon Press, 1979).

Halberstam, David, *The Reckoning* (Avon Books, 1986).

Hayes, Robert H., and William J. Abernathy, "Managing Our Way to Economic Decline," *Harvard Business Review* (July-August, 1980): 67–77.

Hill, Charles W. l., Michael Hitt, and Robert E. Hoskisson "Declining Competitiveness: Reflections on a Crisis," *The Academy of Management Executive*, Vol. 2, No. 1 (1988): 51–60.

Johnson, H. Thomas, and Robert S. Kaplan, *Relevance Lost, The Rise and Fall of Management Accounting* (Harvard Business School Press, 1987).

Kagono, Tadao, I. Nonaka, K. Sakakibara, and A. Okumura, *Strategic vs. Evolutionary Management, A U.S.-Japan Comparison of Strategy and Organization* (North-Holland, 1985).

Kanter, Rosabeth Moss, *When Giants Learn to Dance* (Simon and Schuster, 1989).

Kaplan, Robert S., " Accounting Lag: The Obsolescence of Cost Accounting Systems," *California Management Review*, Vol. 28, No. 2 (Winter, 1986): 174–199.

Katz, Daniel, and Robert L. Kahn, *The Social Psychology of Organizations* (John Wiley & Sons, Inc., 1966).

Khandwalla, Pradip N., "The Effect of Different Types of Competition on the Use of Management Controls," *Journal of Accounting Research* (1972): 275–285.

Khandwalla, Pradip N., "Mass Output Orientation of Operations Technology and Organizational Structure," *Administrative Science Quarterly* (1974): 74–97.

Kilmann, Ralph H. *Beyond the Quick Fix; Managing Five Tracks to Organization Success* (Jose-Bass, 1984).

Kuhn, Arthur. *GM Passes Ford*, (Pennsylvania State University Press, 1986)

Labich, Keats, "Boeing Battles to Stay on Top" *Fortune*, (September 28, 1987): 64–72

Lawrence, Paul R., and Jay W. Lorsch, *Organization and Environment* (Richard D. Irwin, Inc., 1969)

Lawrence, Paul R., and Davis Dyer, *Renewing American Industry: Organizing for Efficiency and Adaptation* (Harvard Business School, 1983).

Lincoln, James R., and Mitsuyo Hanada, and Kerry McBride, "Organizational Structures in Japanese and U.S. Manufacturing," *Administrative Science Quarterly*, Vol. 31 (1986): 338–364.

Lorsch, Jay W., and Stephen A. Allen III, *Managing Diversity and Interdependence* (Harvard University, Graduate School of Business Administration, 1973).

March, James G., "Ambiguity and Accounting: The Elusive Link Between Information and Decision Making," *Accounting, Organizations and Society*, Vol. 12, No. 2 (1987): 153–168.

Means, Grady E. "The CFO, Information Flow, and Global Competition," *Financial Executive* (September/October, 1987): 26–32.

Melman, Seymour, *Production Without Profits* (Random House, 1983).

Meyer, John W., "Social Environments and Organizational Accounting," *Accounting, Organizations and Society* (1986): 345–356.

Miles, Matthew B., and A. Michael Huberman, *Qualitative Data Analysis: A Sourcebook of New Methods* (Sage Publications, 1984).

Miles, Raymond E., Charles C. Snow, Alan D. Meyer, and Henry J. Coleman, Jr., "Organizational Strategy, Structure and Process," *Academy of Management Review*, Vol. 3, No. 3 (July, 1978): 546–562.

Miller, Danny, "Toward a New Contingency Approach: The Search for Organizational Gestalts," *Journal of Management Studies*, Vol. 18, No. 1 (1981): 1–26.

Miller, Danny, and Peter H. Friesen, "Innovation in Conservative and Entrepreneurial Firms," *Strategic Management Journal*, Vol. 3 (1982): 1–25.

Miller, Danny, "The Genesis of Configuration," *Academy of Management Review*, Vol. 12, No. 4 (1987): 686–701.

Miller, Danny, and Peter H. Friesen, *Organizations, A Quantum View* (Prentice-Hall, 1984).

Miller, Danny, and Henry Mintzberg, "The Case for Configuration," in Gareth Morgan (ed.), *Beyond Method* (Sage Publications, 1983): 57–73.

Mintzberg, Henry, *The Structuring of Organizations* (Prentice-Hall, 1979).

Mintzberg, Henry, "An Emerging Theory of 'Direct' Research," in John Van Maanen (ed.) *Qualitative Methodology* (Sage Publications, 1979):

Mintzberg, Henry, "Strategy Formation in an Adhocracy," *Administrative Science Quarterly*, Vol. 30, No.2 (1985): 160–197.

Mueller, Gerhard G., and John K. Simmons, "Change in Accounting Education," *Issues in Accounting Education* (Fall, 1989): 247–251.

Ouchi, William G., "A Conceptual Framework for the Design of Organizational Control Mechanisms," *Management Science*, Vol. 25, No. 9 (September, 1979): 833–848.

Ouchi, William G., "Efficient Cultures: Exploring the Relationship between Culture and Organizational Performance," *Administrative Science Quarterly*, Vol. 28 (1983): 468–481.

Peirce, James L., "The New Image of Controllership," *Financial Executive* (January, 1963): 13–39.

Peters, Thomas J., and Nancy Austin, *A Passion for Excellence: The Leadership Difference* (Random House, 1985).

Peters, Thomas J., and Robert H. Waterman, Jr., *In Search of Excellence* (Warner Books, 1982).

Pfeffer, Jeffrey, *Organizations and Organization Theory* (Pitman, 1982).

Pfeffer, Jeffrey, and Gerald R. Salancik, *The External Control of Organizations* (Harper & Row, 1978).

Pharmaceutical Panel Committee. *The Competitive Status of the US Pharmaceutical Industry.* (National Academy Press, 1983).

Porter, Michael E., *Competitive Strategy* (The Free Press, 1980).

Piore, Michael J. and Charles F. Sabel. *The Second Industrial Divide: Possibility for Prosperity,* (Basic Books 1984).

Reich, Robert B. *The Next American Frontier* (Times Books, 1983).

Reich, Robert B. *Tales of a New America* (Times Books, 1987).

Robbins, Sidney M., and Robert B. Stobaugh, "Growth of the Financial Control Function," *Financial Executive* (July, 1973): 24–31.

Rosenzweig, Kenneth, "An Exploratory Field Study of the Relationship Between the Controller's Department and Overall Organizational Characteristics," *Accounting, Organizations and Society,* Vol. 6, No. 4 (1981): 339–354.

Ross, Barbara, "Technology: How Is it Changing the CFOs Job?" *Financial Executive* (May, 1986): 21–24.

Rushing, William A., "Organizational Size and Administration" The Problems of Causal Homogeneity and a Heterogeneous Category," *Pacific Sociological Review,* Vol. 9 (1966): 100–108.

Sathe, Vijay, *Controllership in Divisionalized Firms: Structure, Evaluation, and Development* (AmaCom, 1978).

Sathe, Vijay, *Controller Involvement in Management* (Prentice-Hall, 1982).

Schlesinger, Leonard. *Chronicles of Corporate Change: Management Lessons form AT&T and Its Offsprings.* (Lexington Books, 1987).

Scott, W. Richard, *Organizations: Rational, Natural and Open Systems* (Prentice-Hall, 1987).

Simon, H.A., and G. Kosmetzsky, H. E. Geutzkow, and T. Tyndall, *Centralization vs. Decentralization in Organizing the Controllership Department* (The Controllership Foundation, 1954).

Simons, Robert, "Accounting Control Systems and Business Strategy: An Empirical Analysis," *Accounting, Organizations and Society,* Vol. 12, No. 4 (1987): 357–374.

Simons, Robert, "Planning, Control and Uncertainty: A Process View," in William J. Bruns, Jr., and Robert S. Kaplan (eds.), *Accounting & Management, Field Study Perspectives* (Harvard Business School Press, 1987): 339–362

Snow Charles C., and Lawrence Hrebiniak, "Strategy, Distinctive Competence, and Organizational Performance," *Administrative Science Quarterly*, Vol. 25 (June, 1980): 317–335.

Thompson, James D. and Arthur Tuden, "Strategies, Structures, and Processes of Organizational Design," in James D. Thompson et al. (eds.), *Comparative Studies in Administration* (University of Pittsburgh Press, 1959).

Thompson, James D. *Organizations in Action* (McGraw-Hill, 1967).

Tiessen, P. and Waterhouse, J. H., "Towards a Descriptive Theory of Management Accounting," *Accounting, Organizations and Society* Vol. 8, No. 2 (1983): 251–267.

Turnstalle, Brooke W., "Cultural Transition at AT&T" *Sloan Management Review* (Fall, 1983): 15–26

Waterman, Robert H. Jr., *The Renewal Factor* (Bantam Books, 1987).

Williams, Kathy, "The Magic of 3M: Management Accounting Excellence," *Management Accounting* (February 1986).

Winograd, Terry, and Fernando Flores, *Understanding Computers and Cognition* (Addison-Wesley, 1987).

Yoshino, M.Y., "Global Competition in a Salient Industry: The Case of Civil Aircraft," in Michael E. Porter, (ed.), *Competition in Global Industries* (Harvard University Business School Press, 1986): 517–538

Zand, D. E., *Information, Organization and Power: Effective Management in the Knowledge Society* (McGraw-Hill, 1981).

References on Research Philosophy, Design and Method

Bernstein, Richard J., *The Restructuring of Social and Political Theory* (University of Pennsylvania Press, 1976).

Blumer, Herbert, "Methodological Principles of Empirical Science," in Norman Denzin (ed.), *Sociological Methods: A Sourcebook* (McGraw-Hill, 1978).

Brinberg, David, and Joseph E. McGrath, "A Network of Validity Concepts Within the Research Process," in Brinberg, David, and Louise H. Kidder (eds.), *New Directions for Methodology of Social and Behavioral Science: Forms of Validity in Research* (Jossey-Bass, 1982):5–21.

Bruns, William J. Jr., and Robert S. Kaplan (eds.), *Accounting & Management, Field Study Perspectives* (Harvard Business School Press, 1987).

Dallmayr, Fred R., and Thomas McCarthy, *Understanding and Social Inquiry* (University of Notre Dame Press, 1977).

Douglas, Jack, D. *Investigative Social Research* (Sage Publications, 1976).

Eckstein, Harry, "Case Study and Theory in Political Science," in Fred I. Greenstein, and Nelson W. Polsby (eds.), *Handbook of Political Science, Vol. 7: Strategies of Inquiry* (Addison-Wesley, 1975): 79–137.

Eisenhardt, Kathleen, "Building Theories from Case Study Research," *Academy of Management Review*, Vol. 14, No. 4 (1989): 532–550.

Fielding Nigel G., and Jane L. Fielding, *Linking Data, the Articulation of Qualitative and Quantitative Methods in Social Research* (Sage Publications, 1986).

Franklin, Clyde W. II, *Theoretical Perspectives in Social Psychology* (Little, Brown and Company, 1982).

Glaser, Barney G., *Theoretical Sensitivity* (Sociology Press, 1978).

Glaser, Barney G., and Anselm L. Strauss, *The Discovery of Grounded Theory: Strategies for Qualitative Research* (Aldine Publishing Co., 1967).

Jick, Todd, "Mixing Qualitative and Quantitative Methods: Triangulation in Action," in John Van Maanen (ed.) *Qualitative Methodology* (Sage, 1979):135–148.

Judd, Charles M., and David A. Kenny, "Research Design and Research Validity," in Brinberg, David, and Louise H. Kidder (eds.), *New Directions for Methodology of Social and Behavioral Science: Forms of Validity in Research* (Jossey-Bass, 1982):5–21.

Kaplan, Robert S., "The Case for Case Studies in Management Accounting Research," (Unpublished Manuscript, 1984).

Kirk, Jerome, and Marc L. Miller, *Reliability and Validity in Qualitative Research* (Sage Publications, 1986).

Lijphart, A., "The Comparative Politics and the Comparative Method," *American Political Science Review*, Vol. 65 (1971): 682–693.

McCall George J., and J. L. Simmons (eds.), *Issues in Participant Observation: A Text and Reader* (Addison-Wesley, 1969).

McKinnon, Jill, "Reliability and Validity in Field Research: Some Strategies and Tactics," *Accounting, Auditing and Accountability*, Vol. 1, No. 1 (1987): 34–44.

Ricoeur, Paul, *Hermeneutics and the Human Sciences* (Cambridge University Press, 1981).

Ricoeur, Paul, *Interpretation Theory* (The Texas Christian University Press, 1976).

Runkel P. J., and J. E. McGrath, *Research on Human Behavior: A Systematic Guide to Method* (Holt, Rhinehart, and Winston, 1972).

Schutz, Alfred, *The Phenomenology of the Social World* (Northwestern University Press, 1967).

Strauss, Anselm L., *Qualitative Analysis for Social Scientists* (Cambridge University Press,1987).

Van Maanen, John (ed.), *Qualitative Methodology* (Sage Publications, 1979).

Weber, Max, *Economy and Society: An Outline of Interpretive Sociology* (Bedminster, 1968).

Yin, Robert K., "The Case Study Crisis: Some Answers," *Administrative Science Quarterly*, Vol. 26 (1981): 58-65.

Yin, Robert K., *Case Study Research, Design and Methods* (Sage Publications, 1984).